VIOLET'S
ARE
Blue

DR. SCOTT ANDREWS

Copyright © 2024 by Dr. Scott Andrews

VIOLET'S ARE *Blue*

All rights reserved. No part of this publication may be reproduced, distributed, or transmitted in any form or by any means, including photocopying, recording, or other electronic or mechanical methods, without the prior written permission of the publisher, except in the case of brief quotations embodied in critical reviews and certain other noncommercial uses permitted by copyright law. For permission requests, write to the publisher, addressed "Attention: Permissions Coordinator," at info@beyondpublishing.net.

Quantity sales and special discounts are available on quantity purchases by corporations, associations, and others. For details, contact the publisher at the address above.

Orders by U.S. trade bookstores and wholesalers email: info@BeyondPublishing.net.

The Beyond Publishing Speakers Bureau can bring authors to your live event. For more information or to book an event contact the Beyond Publishing Speakers Bureau speak@BeyondPublishing.net.

The Author can be reached directly at BeyondPublishing.net.

Manufactured and printed in the United States of America distributed globally by BeyondPublishing.net.

BEYOND
PUBLISHING

New York | Los Angeles | London | Sydney

ISBN Hardcover: 978-1-63792-771-7
ISBN Softcover: 978-1-63792-772-4

TABLE OF CONTENTS

Dedication	5
Introduction	7
Chapter 1 – Our Fairy Tale	9
Journal Journey Except – September 17, 2019	20
Lessons Learned – Don't Sweat The Small Stuff	22
Good Advice – Simplify Your Life	26
Chapter 2 – Violets in Bloom	29
Coping Tools – Professional Counseling	35
Journal Journey Excerpt – September 23, 2022	38
Lessons Learned – Will I Be A Good Parent?	40
Good Advice: Thursday Nights	44
Chapter 3 – Time Stood Still	47
Coping Tools – Faith	55
Journal Journey Excerpt – January 10, 2023	59
Lessons Learned – Give Grace	61
Good Advice – Allow Yourself To Feel	65
Chapter 4 – Shock and Denial	69
Coping Tools – Pets	74
Journal Journey Excerpt – February 25, 2023	76
Lessons Learned – Working Through The Pain	78
Good Advice: Take Back Control of Your Life	81
Chapter 5 – The Reset	84
Coping Tools – Exercise	87
A Journal Journey – The Butterfly	91

  Lessons Learned – Unhealthy Coping   94
  Good Advice: - Get Lost To Find Yourself   98
Chapter 6 – The Weight of Absence   105
  Coping Tools – Indulging   110
  A Journal Journey Excerpt – The Cost of Ambition 113
  Lessons Learned - Sit with the Pain   115
  Good Advice – Fight for Your Happiness, Every Single Day 118
Chapter 7 – Helping Hands   120
  Coping Tools - The Violet Movement   124
  A Journal Journey – July 15, 2023   127
  Lessons Learned – It is Okay to Not be Okay 129
  Good Advice – Seasons Greetings   130
Chapter 8 – Cycles of Life   134
  Coping Tools – The Magic of Nostalgia   137
  A Journal Journey Excerpt – Thanksgiving 2023 141
  Good Advice – Go For It   143
  Lessons Learned – Balancing Act   147
Chapter 9 – Fuzzy   148
  Coping Tools -Writing and Journaling   152
  A Journal Journey Excerpt – Meeting "Jada" 155
  Lessons Learned – A Piercing Lesson   158
  Good Advice – Date Nights   162
Chapter 10 - Miles of Joy   166
Final Reflections   172
References   174

DEDICATION

This book is the culmination of my family's brightest days and darkest hours. It is inspiring, joyful, anxiety laden, painful, and hopeful all at once. Above all it is completely authentic, capturing our human experience during the most challenging years of our lives. This book, "Violet's Are Blue" is intended to honor our daughter Violet Françoise Andrews. However, I would like to dedicate this book to all the parents that have lost a child and know the agony of trying to find your way forward again. There is no pain like it. While there is no path back to "normal," it is absolutely normal to grieve completely different than others that have experienced a similar loss.

This book shares intimate details of our lives. This book is not something we take lightly and it has been very challenging at times to relive some of these moments. It is completely worth it if it helps others through loss, grief, depression and their own struggles with mental health. Everything you are feeling is part of your own journey. We are all in this together. We are so grateful to our family, friends, colleagues, coworkers, neighbors, and communities. We would not be able to share our story without the love and support of so many.

Special thanks to my wife, best friend and partner in life, Danielle. You inspire me to be a better person every single day. You are my favorite; I love you so much. Thank you for tolerating another one of my ideas.

To Violet: We think about you every single day. We love you so much. I hope that we make you proud in our everyday actions. Your name and spirit will live on through others. We know that God has wrapped you with his love and warmth. We will see you again one day.

INTRODUCTION

The past 24 months have been the most tumultuous of our lives. Amidst the rewards and challenges, I kept a detailed journal, a practice that has been therapeutic for me for years. As the months of journaling passed, I felt a growing need to share our story, encouraged by those close to me. This book was born, emerging from the pages of my journals. It is the story of my family, capturing our dreams, defeats, and defining comebacks.

This project isn't just a book; it's a testament to the human spirit's ability to endure, adapt, and ultimately, find its way back to the light after being plunged into darkness. When you lose a child, the world as you know it ends. There's a void, a chasm that swallows you whole. But in that darkness, we found something else. We discovered a resilience we never knew we had, a strength forged in the trials of our deepest pain. This book captures that journey, not just as a recollection of events, but as a map for others who might find themselves lost in the same wilderness of grief. Our goal in sharing this story is multifaceted. It's a raw, honest portrayal of our excitement and anxiousness as first-time parents, the unimaginable grief of losing our daughter Violet, and the slow, painful process of piecing our lives back together. But more than that, it's a call to arms for anyone struggling with their own battles, whether they're facing grief, depression, or simply the trials of life. By candidly sharing our whirlwind of life, death, and rebirth, I hope to offer solace to others navigating similar storms.

Grief is a treacherous trek that many of us will take at some point in our lives, yet it remains one of the most isolating experiences. Society often shies away from discussing the uncomfortable realities of loss, as if by avoiding the topic, we can somehow shield ourselves from the inevitable. The reality is that grief is as much a part of life as joy, and only by facing it head-on can we begin to heal. This book aims to break through the silence that often surrounds grief, to shed light on its darkest corners, and to offer a hand to those who are stumbling through their own painful periods of life. Normalizing conversations about mental health isn't just important, it is necessary. This book is my attempt to walk the talk.

In the chapters ahead, I document our story. You will be a part of our family's rise, spiral, and renewal as we find our new normal after tragedy. Our story is not just about loss, but about the love that has sustained us through it. It's about the community that wrapped its arms around us, the friends and family who stood by us when we couldn't stand on our own, and the moments of grace that came when we least expected them. As our story progresses, I hope the series of sub-sections within the book brings value to those who are currently in the trenches after loss. The chapters are laid out in easy-to-read, digestible subsections that are categorized and detailed within each chapter. Every chapter begins with a brief narrative, written over the last two years, followed by sections that are intended break up the heaviness of the topics discussed. We've included summaries of the good, bad, and ugly, examples of coping tools that worked well and others that failed us. Smile, sigh, reflect, and laugh along with our lessons learned, detailing our passage from grief to growth. Many chapters will end with good advice, shedding light on your own path as you or someone you care about journeys through dark times. Crawl, walk, and rise with us on this intimate passage of heartache and hope.

This journey has been one of profound transformations. Grief has a way of stripping away the layers of who we thought we were, forcing us to confront our most vulnerable selves. But within that vulnerability lies the seed of transformation. The loss of Violet didn't just break us, it forced us to reset who we thought we were. It reshaped our understanding of life, love, and what it means to truly live. In sharing this journey, my hope is to create a space where others can see their own experiences reflected in ours, where they can find comfort in the knowledge that they are not alone.

In the pages that follow, you'll find more than just words; you'll discover the heart and soul of my family's journey through the unimaginable and how this profound experience reshaped every aspect of life. We will candidly pull back the curtain on the window to our lives. We tell the tale of how our once idyllic world was shattered and turned upside down after the traumatic loss of Violet Françoise Andrews. It is my hope that our story balances the rawness of grief with the inspiration drawn from our experiences, ensuring you feel a sense of connection and empathy with your own life.

This is not merely a narrative; it's a testament to love, endurance, and the transformative power of grief. It is a chronicle of our battle with loss, grief, and depression, but also a journal of inspiration, resilience, and the enduring strength of the human spirit. Our journey is proof that even in the face of overwhelming sorrow, there is a way forward, one that honors the memory of those we've lost while finding a renewed purpose in the life that remains.

Grief forces us to face the raw, unvarnished truth of who we are, stripping away the illusions we once held about ourselves and the world. It's in these moments of profound exposure that we discover the potential for growth and change. The loss of Violet didn't merely fracture our lives, it fundamentally altered the way we see the world. It redefined our perceptions of love, purpose, and what it means to continue living after an unimaginable loss. Through this book, my hope is to create a connection with others who are navigating their own struggles, offering a sense of solidarity and understanding. By sharing our story, we aim to show that even in the depths of sorrow, there exists the possibility for renewal and resilience.

In this book, you won't find a step-by-step guide to overcoming grief because grief isn't something you overcome; it's something you survive, and it changes you. Severe grief is something you learn to live with. Instead, you'll find a story of love, loss, and the ways we've managed to piece our lives back together, one day at a time. You'll find the raw, unfiltered truth of what it means to lose a child and the hard-won wisdom that comes from living through that kind of pain. We don't have all the answers, but we hope that by sharing our story, we can offer some comfort to those who are going through their own trials. If there's one thing we've learned, it's that healing is not a destination, it's an epic odyssey. And like any journey, it's easier when you have someone to walk with you. Let this book be your companion, your guide, and your reminder that even in the darkest of times, you are not alone.

CHAPTER 1

Our Fairy Tale

In August of 2018, a happy-go-lucky, adventurous girl from Massachusetts serendipitously "swiped the right way" for an ambitious, kind-hearted Tampa native on the dating app Hinge. Danielle's soft-spoken, gentle nature was a pleasant surprise in the often-raunchy world of online dating. She knows exactly who she is and isn't, and I have always found that so dang refreshing. I was drawn to her sincerity and sense of humor almost immediately. There was something magnetic about the way she carried herself, confident yet humble, with a quiet strength that resonated deeply with me. We would message every day, but both had very busy lives. I would join her after her 12-hour nursing shifts for a quick, dog-walk date with her #1 man, Romeo. These moments, though fleeting, were like little windows into a future that I couldn't wait to step into. Even in those early days, I sensed that something extraordinary was unfolding.

Danielle and I had both been through long-term relationships that didn't go quite as planned. Danielle had only one ring; she didn't have to go through the other two. Meanwhile, I had dealt with all three rings; the engagement ring, the wedding ring, and the suffer-ring that came with my starter marriage. I'm fairly confident that Danielle didn't know what to make of me at first. However, I was honest, persistent, and she continued to be intrigued enough for me to slowly reel her in. Danielle had a big trip planned with a friend to England and Iceland. I remember wanting to be there with her so much, but also being so proud of her for seeing the world. We talked almost daily while she was away. Each conversation felt like a puzzle piece clicking into place, slowly revealing the picture of what our life could look like together.

I loved hearing about her explorations each day, and we continued to bond while she was away. There's a unique magic that comes from sharing stories of distant lands with someone who listens intently, who sees the world with the same sense of wonder. Every time she described a new sight, a new experience, it felt like I was right there with her, exploring the unknown. I admired and connected with her more by the week. Danielle and I love to travel for the experience of being entrenched in a place. We can't stand the idea of going to an all-inclusive or visiting a new country just to say we've been there. We crave the culture, adventure, traditions, cuisine, and the deeper connection that comes from submerging ourselves in a new environment. The best classrooms do not have four walls, and for us, the world is our classroom.

When Danielle returned from her big trip, things escalated quickly, as they typically do when people in their 30s find something real. We were an item, dating, and official on social media within a few more weeks. It was like our souls recognized each other, and the speed at which we became a couple felt like the most natural progression in the world. We started meeting each other's close friends, and by November, we had met each other's families for our first holiday season together. There's a saying that you don't really know your partner until you have traveled with them or lived with them. I would definitely say that held true with us, as we had an amazing time on our first big trip together. Guatemala isn't a place that most would list as where they want to go for their first strip together. However, it was a fantastic deal, offered unique cultural opportunities and we were eager to explore together. It was there, amid the ancient ruins and vibrant landscapes, that I began to see the depth of Danielle's spirit. She has a distinct way of processing decisions and life moments. Once she does, she embraces the unknown. Her ability to find joy in the simplest of moments is one of my favorite traits she possesses.

However, we had some growing pains as we moved in together with four pets in our 1,000-square-foot Atlanta condo. It's a good thing I take care of myself and have a great career because she definitely was not purr-suaded by my three cats and 700-square-foot apartment. As much as we were in sync, there were still the inevitable adjustments that come with blending two lives. We both love our animals so abundantly and truly see them as furry family members. We had to work through the feline trio of Rodney, Simon, and Stella not immediately meshing well with Danielle and the OG Golden Doodle, Romeo. After a few cat-tastrophes, we found our new normal together in the heart of Midtown ATL. Looking back, those moments were both challenging and endearing, tiny tests of our compatibility. It wasn't always a picture perfect life, but we were enjoying the ride while growing as a couple.

Adventure has always been a big part of my life as well. When Danielle and I met, I also had a big trip booked and planned for myself. I was so excited for the incredible deal I got to go to the Netherlands, Germany, Belgium, and Luxembourg. Little did I know that this solo adventure would turn into something far more significant. Danielle would end up accompanying me on the European getaway, and what I initially thought would be a trip for my inner growth turned into monumental moments in our story.

It's funny how life takes you by surprise when you least expect it. My trip to Northern Europe was supposed to be about character development and finding myself again. Instead, I found myself proposing to my girlfriend. The idea of spending my life with Danielle had taken root so deeply in my heart after our trip to Guatemala. Proposing felt like the only logical step forward. I anxiously carried an engagement ring in my pocket and had even hired a photographer to await us at an iconic bridge in Amsterdam at a particular time so they could capture our moment. Well, a torrential rain downpour began just before, and the proposal was mentally postponed for me that day. I am not sure if she even knew how stressed I was that day as things did not go according to plan. But in hindsight, I realize that love isn't about perfect moments; it's about the imperfect ones that make the journey unforgettable. I wasn't expecting to get a negative response, and admittedly Danielle would have been content with almost any proposal, but I wanted it to be unique. The moment had to be special for this amazing woman who was, and is, my favorite person on Earth.

The next day brought better weather and new opportunities as we navigated our way to Cologne, Germany. However, the travel planner in me already had the rest of the week booked up. Thus, it would take some creativity and timing to pull off a proposal that I was beginning to put too high on the psychological pedestal. I had already organized a jam-packed day, with a city tour followed by a brewery tour in the evening. I mean, when in Germany…you do as the Germans do. At the end of the night, we concluded our beer tour by enjoying a few Kölsch beers, which are native only to Cologne, or Köln as the locals call it.

During our brewery tour, we hit it off with a couple of travel nurses that happened to be on the same hoppy excursion as us. When Danielle got up to go to the restroom, I told them that I had the engagement ring in my pocket. I asked if they would help record our moment if I proposed in front of the stunning Köln cathedral on the walk out. They were ecstatic to take part in the fun. They recorded me, teeth chattering from nerves and the 28-degree January weather in Germany. Have you ever had one of those moments where you just felt like you would be okay, no matter what life threw at you? This was that moment for me. I stood there, paused, then got down on one knee. The woman I love said "yes" in front of one of the most breathtaking cathedrals in the world. I knew from that moment forward that we would have an amazing life together.

We had a fair number of ups and downs, as any new relationship does, but we always seemed to agree on the big things. After being engaged for a few weeks, we both realized that we had no interest in a big wedding. We were more interested in growing our relationship, exploring new countries, and avoiding all the drama that comes with wedding planning. My beautiful, no-nonsense fiancée and I made the decision to get married abroad. The money that we would have spent on a wedding went towards our pilgrimage to Italy, Israel, Greece, and Malta. Danielle purchased a wedding dress on Amazon, packed it up, and we proceeded to celebrate our fairy tale in our unique way. We exchanged our vows, overlooking the majestic columns and relics of the Roman Forum, as a small audience of strangers looked on. It was as if history itself was bearing witness to our union, reminding us that love, like the ancient ruins around us, is something that endures through time and trials.

We celebrated the evening by walking around the streets of Rome in our wedding attire. Danielle somehow made the Trevi Fountain radiate even brighter that evening. Our history was sealed at one of the most historic and romantic places on Earth. Two would become one. Our passions, purpose, and paths were now set in stone, setting the stage for the amazing life we would share together. Looking back, it's clear that our love story wasn't just about the moments of joy and celebration, but also about the challenges we faced together. The decisions, big and small, that brought us closer and strengthened our bond.

This chapter of our lives was the foundation upon which we would build our future. Each moment, each adventure, each challenge, was a brick in the home we were creating together. It was a period of discovery, of the world, of each other, and of ourselves. As we moved forward, hand in hand, we knew that whatever lay ahead, we would face it together. Our love was not just a fleeting romance but a deep, enduring connection that would guide us through the years to come.

Journal Journey: September 17, 2019

As a reminder, this subsection of the book is a peek behind the curtain of my mind. I am an open book and am a firm believer in the power of journaling. The idea of this book came from some of the positive feedback that I received after sharing a few of my journal entries on social media over the past few years. Now that you know the genesis for this subsection, here is the first Journal Journey entry from September 17, 2019. This was the day after our incredible Roman wedding.

Amid the shadows of an ancient world, we stood together at the epicenter of the Roman empire, hearts intertwined, on the cusp of forever. There, with the storied ruins of the Roman Forum bearing witness, we exchanged vows that were as timeless as the city itself. Danielle looked incredible, the embodiment of so many dreams I have had manifesting itself to my amazement. This was our fairy tale, our moment suspended in the eternal city where all roads led to a shared future. It was a day of joy, an affirmation that love, in all its forms, is the truest conquest. As I held Danielle, and felt the soft rustle of her wedding dress, I knew that our journey together would be one of grand adventure, shared aspirations, and of a love that would dare to dance among the echoes of history.

The majestic ruins around us were a testament to the enduring pulse of life through the ages. They reminded us that while empires rise and fall, the truest legacy is the love we give, the kindness we share, and the lives we touch. On that day, the past and present converged. Our hearts spoke a silent promise to honor the beauty of life's impermanence, to cherish each fleeting moment, and to lead our lives with a love as enduring as the cobblestones beneath our feet.

Our fairy tale Roman wedding set the stage for the depths of love we would come to know. It was a beginning painted in hope and light, a canvas upon which we would later understand the stark contrasts of life, the unyielding joy of love, and the profound sorrow of loss.

Yet, that day in Rome, as the sun set over the eternal city, everything felt possible. The challenges of the future, unknown and unknowable, seemed distant, mere whispers against the roar of our love. Standing there with Danielle, I felt invincible. The world was ours, and the journey ahead, however uncertain, was one we would face together. The little moments of this big day still stand out to me. Watching Danielle write her wedding vows, in her dress, all in one take. The strangers clapping for us, congratulating and wishing us well. Borrowing the roses from the street vendor for the photo opportunity in front of the Trevi Fountain. Meandering the winding cobblestone streets and enjoying amazing treats at the shops along the way. The memory of that day, frozen in time, would later become a beacon in the dark days that followed, a reminder of the love that sparked it all.

Lessons Learned – Don't Sweat the Small Stuff

"Don't sweat the small stuff" is a phrase that many wise mentors have echoed over the years. It's shared for good reason, but as with most advice, it's much easier to understand in hindsight. Life has a way of forcing us to reflect, and it's only after we've climbed a few mountains that the pebbles we once stumbled over seem so insignificant. When you're in the thick of merging lives with someone you love, those small things can feel like enormous obstacles. The majority of this book will focus on more recent, impactful, and obviously more important challenges, but all of these early relationship lessons seem so trivial now. They serve as a reminder that even the small, seemingly inconsequential moments in life can teach us something valuable.

So, with a smirk and an eye roll, I lighten the mood and set the stage for our first lessons learned subsection, which focuses on some of the early relationship struggles and seemingly inconsequential things in retrospection that may be a headache for some new couples. Pets are furry family members to Danielle and I; we love the heck out of them and treat them like our children. When two parents feel they are watching over their children, and the kids aren't getting along, it can get testy. Do you know why an Instapot works so much faster than a crockpot? It's the insane pressure that heats things up really quickly. We crammed three cats, a 60 lb. dog, and two stubborn adults into 1,000 square feet. We were living the Instapot life. I never had a dog as an adult, and Danielle never owned a cat. It was a good thing I was running a buy-one-cat, get-two-free special.

Those early days of living together were a whirlwind of adjustments. We had just moved in together, bringing our respective furry companions under one roof. The tiny space magnified every little quirk and habit. Danielle had Romeo, her beloved golden doodle, and I had Rodney, Simon, and Stella, the feline trio who believed they ruled the world. Neither of us was particularly prepared for the chaos that would ensue. The cats, of course, were not thrilled about sharing their domain with a dog, and Romeo wasn't exactly thrilled about being outnumbered by cats. Our home, though filled with love, became a battleground where the animals, and occasionally we, ought for territory.

We were trying to establish a new normal, and sometimes it felt like we were failing at it. Simple things like feeding time turned into a choreographed dance to prevent any "accidental" run-ins between Romeo and the cats. It was a test of patience for both of us. There were nights when we'd be exhausted from our respective jobs, only to come home and find that one of the cats had taken over Romeo's favorite spot on the couch, or that Romeo had decided the litter box was an interesting place to explore. The stress of those early days often led to bickering, but in hindsight, they were lessons in compromise.

Neither one of us is into material things too much, but we bickered a lot over furniture when we moved in together. We found ourselves clashing over silly things, like which pieces of furniture would stay and which would go. Anyone else remember squabbling over which furniture was being kept, and what is being donated or trashed? By squabble, I mean I made a few good arguments but ultimately lost. I ended up getting rid of my sofa and loveseat that day. I didn't even like the stuff that much; it just became sentimental to me because it was my first major purchase as an adult. But that's the thing about relationships, sometimes you have to let go of the things you think matter to make room for the things that truly do.

The sofa and loveseat didn't stand a chance against Danielle's practicality. Looking back, I can laugh at how much weight I gave to those pieces of furniture. It wasn't about the furniture itself; it was about what it represented to me, independence, adulthood, and the life I had built before Danielle came into it. But letting go of those things wasn't a loss. It was a gain in the form of a stronger relationship, one that was learning to prioritize the people in it over the possessions. I lost that argument but not my girlfriend turned wife. I'd say I did okay on that decision in the long run. Sarcasm aside, this is often what we do, though; we give so much sentiment to possessions. Relationships and people often take a backseat to projects, professions, and the pursuit of pesos. Whether you giggled at my expense during this example or because you remember being in a similar situation, we can't forget the age-old lesson that we started with: don't sweat the small stuff. Focus on what truly matters, bypass the petty, and embrace the profound.

But beyond the jokes and the banter lies a deeper truth. In those moments of seemingly trivial disputes, we were laying the foundation for something much greater. The ability to compromise, to let go of the small things, and to focus on the bigger picture were lessons we were unknowingly preparing ourselves for. These early tests of our relationship were the training ground for the challenges we would later face. They taught us resilience, patience, and the importance of choosing love over being right. And in the grand scheme of life, it's those choices that define the strength of a relationship.

Over time, we learned that the disagreements over furniture and the battles between pets were not the end of the world, but rather, the beginning of our journey together. They were the first steps in a long dance of learning to live with each other's quirks, preferences, and pasts. They were the small stuff that, at the moment, seemed so significant but in reality, were just minor bumps on the road to building a life together. And now, as I look back, I can see how those early days, with all their challenges and compromises, were crucial in shaping the strong partnership we have today.

Good Advice - Be Positive and Simplify Your Life

If you have ever seen the movie *Deadpool*, you'll likely remember the hilariously famous scene where Wade (Deadpool) meets Vanessa for the first time. They have a hysterically positive dialogue about horrific things in their past. "I slept in a dishwasher box," exclaims Vanessa. Wade quips back, "You had a dishwasher?"

The two characters continue to go back and forth, exchanging awful, inappropriate stories from their childhood. Their banter serves as a masterclass in perspective, because sometimes, the only thing more therapeutic than a good cry is a good laugh. The moral of this example is that they keep their sense of humor. When life hands you hardships and challenges, it is critically important to simplify your life and focus on what you do have.

Imagine if we could channel our inner Deadpool when faced with our own less-than-ideal moments. Instead of dwelling on the "dishwasher" we never had, let's appreciate the "box" for what it represents: resilience, creativity, and the simple, undeniable fact that we are still here, still kicking, and still capable of joy. So, let's take a leaf out of Wade's hilariously illustrated book and keep our sense of humor as sharp as his swords.

Nestled amongst tales of trials and triumphs in this book lies a playful nudge towards gratitude even when the going gets tough, think Deadpool tough. Yes, our charmingly cheeky anti-hero, Wade Wilson, has a thing or two to teach us about keeping spirits high in the face of adversity. Amidst the gray skies of grief and loss, let's not forget the power of a good laugh. Simplify your life by decluttering the unnecessary woes, and focus on the silver linings, like the fact that we live in a world where Ryan Reynolds can deliver life lessons while wearing a spandex suit. Be like Deadpool: when the odds are against you, when the days seem grim, put on that figurative superhero suit, crack a joke, even if it's just for yourself, and face the world with a wink and a smile. It might not fix everything, but it'll make the journey a heck of a lot more enjoyable for everyone involved.

But beyond the humor, there's a deeper lesson to be learned. Life is complicated enough without us adding to the chaos. The art of simplifying isn't about denying the complexities but rather choosing to focus on what truly matters. It's about stripping away the noise, the distractions, and the endless list of "should haves" that society throws at us. It's about finding joy in the little things and holding onto those moments of happiness with both hands. Because at the end of the day, it's not the big events that shape us, it's the small, everyday choices we make that determine the quality of our lives.

CHAPTER 2

Violet Is In Bloom

Those who know Danielle and I well are aware that working with youth is a shared passion for us. My journey in local government began as a coach and personal trainer focused on working with teens. My first government job as a Fitness Coordinator was certainly a non-traditional path to City/County Management. Ironically, my next two promotions in Parks and Recreation stemmed from mentoring, coaching, and working with teens and youth. Danielle's foundation is similar, built on working with youth. She has been a nurse for 18 years, with over 16 of those years dedicated to the demanding role of a pediatric cardiac ICU nurse, expertly managing heart bypass machines for some of the most critically ill children in the United States. I regret that we have only seen glimpses of each other's interaction and bonds with youth. I have seen the powerful bonds she has with youth (and their families). Most (good) spouses think that their partner is a saint. It is always nice when everyone agrees with you. I honestly cant think of anyone that doesn't like my wife.

We both found our sense of community, our careers, our work families, and our callings through a foundation built on serving the next generation. I have always found that very intriguing even though we have never discussed it. The team at Children's Healthcare of Atlanta helped raise Danielle from a young woman to a leader in her profession. Meanwhile, I was aligning myself with mentors across the country and working to diversify my background in local government in hopes of one day serving as a City Manager. My first 11 years in local government were in the Parks and Recreation department, a niche where I felt very loved but was pigeonholed for the first portion of my career.

Working with youth has always been deeply rewarding for both of us. There is a unique satisfaction that comes from being able to mentor, guide, and influence the next generation. It's a role that requires patience, empathy, and a deep sense of responsibility, qualities that Danielle has cultivated over the years. Yet, despite my mentality and experiences, the thought of becoming a father terrified me. This fear wasn't just a passing thought; it was deeply rooted in my childhood, my past life, and the belief that after prioritizing my career for so long, I was too old to be a dad. The irony is that I had actively avoided fatherhood for my entire life, decades spent making an intentional choice not to be a father. Danielle, on the other hand, was born to be a mother. It's in her DNA. She can swaddle and change diapers in her sleep. In contrast, I have held about four children in my life and, to this day, haven't changed a single diaper.

Danielle and I had both been in serious relationships in the past, and we were both on the wrong side of heartache in our past lives. When we met, neither of us defined any aspect of our lives as a success or failure by not having children. We were content with the life we were building together, regardless of whether or not it included children. In addition to Danielle, I had several trusted friends who made me more open-minded to the idea of having children. We weren't hung up on the idea of trying for a child; we left it in God's hands. Danielle had her birth control device removed, we prayed, and we let God do the rest.

    I'll never forget the day that our lives changed forever, when our dreams became a reality. It was a springtime Georgia evening, and Danielle called out from the other room, "Come here." I was super comfortable and reluctant to move, but the second "Come here, babe" followed with a more serious tone. I marched into the other room like any other well-trained husband would. "Sit down," she exclaimed with a serious, straight face. My mind immediately began to race, wondering what terrible thing had happened. My thoughts went to dark places, I feared that a loved one was very sick or had passed away. Then her mask wore off, and her smile surfaced as she held the positive pregnancy test. A palpable mix of disbelief and elation raced through us like it has for so many new parents before us. The room was filled with a profound energy and a sense of wonder, as if we were stepping into a new realm.

    We embraced and laughed as my mind raced through dozens of scenarios. Our hearts were overwhelmed with a love that was both new and ancient, a love for a child we had yet to meet but already felt an unbreakable bond with. We imagined the possibilities, the adventures, the laughter, and the love that would fill our home with the arrival of our baby. The world, in that instant, seemed brighter, full of promise and joy. It was every emotion all at once, then the sum of those feelings multiplied by 2,200. That's a pretty specific number, and it reflects how many miles away my new job would be. Just one week prior, I had accepted a job offer in California.

It was my biggest promotion and job title to date. I was going to be a dad. In the weeks that followed, we bought a house, sold a house, packed all our belongings, and said our farewells to all our Atlanta-area friends. It was bittersweet, tiresome, and stressful as hell. I loaded up my pregnant wife, hyper puppy, and three very unsure cats. Even though I had never driven an RV before, we embraced our adventurous sides and embarked on a cross-country journey from Atlanta to Bakersfield, CA. The open road from Atlanta was our canvas, and our RV the brush. We painted our path with love, laughter, and anticipation. We bought matching, themed shirts for each day, mapped out our trek, researched restaurants, and made our trip into a true adventure. That is the Andrews way. We made amazing memories and friends along our path to providence. We stopped every 8 to 10 hours for two days at a time to explore new destinations along our passage. We arrived at our new home in Bakersfield a week later, exhausted but energized.

Danielle had not seen our new house in person yet, so I was on edge until I got to see her reactions to our new home. Her smiles put me at ease, though. We began discussing and visualizing where our furniture would go and where some of our favorite items would be placed. We peeked into every cabinet and each room. We spent several minutes in the smallest bedroom, which felt cozy and intimate, with the perfect amount of western-facing windows. The sunset leaked in the ideal amount of light for our plants and child to bloom in the nursery. A few more weeks passed, and we began getting to know our neighbors and colleagues better. We felt welcomed and supported by our new community. We couldn't believe all the generous housewarming gifts we received from complete strangers. We were amazed by the kindness of our new friends and neighbors, who hosted a gender reveal for us.

On September 25th, our excitement reached a palpable frenzy. As we opened a cardboard box gender reveal prop, pink balloons floated out, and we now knew we were having a baby girl. She was developing an identity and personality in our minds as we began to visualize a life with our daughter. I imagined "Daddy's little girl." My mind conjured up images of me with her at Daddy-Daughter dances, embarrassing her in middle school, intimidating her first few boyfriends, and wrapping my brain around the thought of being the father of the bride one day. In the meantime, it was time to figure out what all these gadgets and baby electronics are, and how to work that darn car seat.

To say that I was excited would be a monumental understatement. I went out and purchased three different "girl dad" shirts that still rotate through my regular wardrobe. I wrote poems and songs for Violet (included in the book's appendix) about her parents and how we visualized making memories with our child. I looked for any opportunity to paint Danielle's pregnant belly, with my favorite design being a basketball, as we wore our matching Shaq and Penny jerseys. Then there was the nursery. We kept it very gender-neutral with a childlike safari theme. After a recent trip to Kenya and Tanzania, it seemed too perfect of a theme not to run with. Sitting atop the wallpaper that Danielle installed during a nesting fury was the delicate, cursive wall art spelling out Violet's name. Across from the crib and her namesake wall art were cartoon-themed safari animals nestled in three different frames. For some reason, the giraffe, elephant, and lion wall art always stood out to me. I envisioned creating stories about the animal characters and reading them to Violet. I could not have been more thrilled to meet our little girl.

The happiness we experienced upon learning of Violet's impending arrival is a crucial part of our story and this book. This chapter offers a glimpse into the intense emotions that accompany the journey of parenthood in all its forms. As you navigate through this chapter with us, I invite you to feel the fullness of our happiness, to immerse yourself in the memory of anticipation and hope. It's a testament to the fact that even in the face of impending sorrow, moments of pure joy are not just fleeting memories; they are the foundation of our love, the first brushstrokes in the vibrant painting of Violet's life.

Coping Tool: Professional Counseling

The "Coping Tools" sub-section of the book is dedicated to sharing the good, bad, and ugly outcomes of coping methods based on our experiences. In future sections, I'll highlight a few less traditional suggestions. However, I want to start off with a few expert-recommended methods that are mutually agreed upon for a reason. I have grown up with family members who have battled some pretty severe mental health issues in my life. I have visited loved ones in mental health institutions on several occasions. I have felt and seen what happens when life overpowers people you love. I have also experienced what happens when you don't prioritize your mental health. Thus, I must admit that I see mental health a bit differently than most.

As a former personal trainer, people would hire me to work with them for 3 to 6 months to help them address being overweight, out of shape, or in poor physical health. Our progress would often vary on how much work they put in when we weren't together. Why should we treat our mental health any differently? I see mental health as a fluid ebb and flow. Good and bad things happen in life, and we must be able to balance and juggle several different aspects of our lives.

I am open-minded and self-aware enough to know that I was stressed to the max with all the big life changes we were facing after the cross-country move and awaiting our daughter, as a first time father on the wrong side of 40. Even pregnant and facing a rush of hormones, Danielle is much more mild-mannered than I am. I am deeply passionate, super ambitious, and very hard on myself. Saying all of that, I could tell by how irritable and moody I was becoming on the weekends that I needed to find a mental health advocate in our new community. I was starting to feel crushed by the career, social, family, and financial expectations I was putting on myself. I knew that I couldn't run the risk of taking it out on the person that I love the most. Understanding the value of professional guidance has been a crucial part of my journey. Thus, it was time to lean on one of my battle-tested and favorite coping tools.

I highly recommend talking through complex and personal challenges with a therapist, as they offer a lot of professional insight that even the most trusted friends cannot satisfy. Personally speaking, sometimes you don't even want to hear a friend's opinion, you just want someone to listen without any judgement. This is an area of extreme value to me in utilizing a counselor. I have had counselors most of my life to help cope with different, unfortunate life events over the years. I have no negative stigmas or worldviews associated with seeing a counselor. I practiced what I preach and started talking to a counselor about my fears of being an older, first-time dad. It gave me a safe space to talk out loud about many of my apprehensions and worries about how I would be able to balance being a good husband, father, leader, and all the other roles I play. I was also able to share many selfish thoughts that I might be hesitant to share with a friend. How would we continue to travel the way we want? Will I still be able to get enough sleep and go to the gym every day? If you are reading this as a parent, you'll likely chuckle at my expense, but looking back, we all know we thought about things like this at some point. Using a counselor helps to talk through vulnerable thoughts like this openly without any fear of judgment.

For anyone grappling with grief, uncertainty, or life transitions, professional counseling can be a lifeline. It offers a perspective outside our immediate experience, provides coping strategies, and most importantly, offers the reassurance that we are not alone in our struggles. I highly encourage others to value and seek professional counseling in times of need. It's about breaking down the stigmas associated with therapy and recognizing that mental health care is a vital component of our overall well-being. I share this aspect of my journey to emphasize the importance of being open-minded and perceptive to the need for professional help. It's a testament to the fact that preparing for life's challenges, including those we cannot foresee, involves recognizing when we need support beyond our personal resources. Whether it's an ongoing part of life or a response to specific challenges, professional support can be a powerful coping tool in our arsenal for healing, growing, and responding to life's challenges.

Journal Journey: September 23, 2022

This spoken word poem is deeply personal and reflects all the emotions that a first-time father has while eagerly anticipating their firstborn. This poem has grown to mean more to me recently, as we progress in our story. Let's get the vulnerability express rolling. As a reminder, this was written for our first born several months before she was born. At 2 ½ months before delivery date, we still did not know gender at this stage.

"Hey there Baby A

We can't wait to see you in about 100 days!

We're still not sure if you'll be a boy or a girl,

But I can promise you that you're our whole world.

We're having a baby!

Omg! So scary, so fun.
It's the greatest thing we've ever done.
We've taken our love, manifested a dream,
From two… we'll soon be a party of three.
Seeing your ultrasound was a blessing, an important lesson.
Our priorities shifted that second, the next step in life's progression.
At the moment I cut your umbilical cord,
The heavens will know a star is born.
When I first look into your eyes,
I'm going to try really hard not to cry.
From the first breath you breathe
and when you first smile at me,
I hope you realize and believe,
you can be anything you want to be.
You'll be so much better than me
because the love of our family runs so very deep.
Through our love, you will achieve, unlike your mom,
I never had you inside me,
But having you as my child will be like my heart
walking beside me.
Praise God, the keeper of the stars,
He sure knew what he was doing
when he joined our two hearts.
I know I'll hold everything, when they place you in my arms.

Never be alarmed as we will never let you be harmed,
Sent to us from God you're our good luck charm.
We are both so happy that you will soon exist.
If you're anything like your mother, you'll be hard to resist.
I hope I make you proud, that I am your father every day.
Because, you have filled our dreams in more ways than any words can say.
I have been reflecting a lot lately, more so now than I ever have,
I hope you love your mother
as much as she is loved by your Dad.
I'm scared and excited, even anxious, I've been told,
We're going to be a family, and our baby we will soon hold."

Lessons Learned – Will I Be a Good Parent?

This is the question that haunted my thoughts, whispered in the quiet moments, and echoed in the conversations I had with myself and others. It wasn't just a passing worry; it was a persistent, nagging doubt. I even asked close friends, not because I expected them to have all the answers, but because I needed reassurance that my fears weren't unfounded. The idea of fatherhood loomed large, casting shadows that were hard to ignore. These weren't just the ordinary shadows of doubt; they were the long, lingering specters of my own childhood, filled with memories that were both cherished and haunting. Those memories seemed to stand as guardians at the gate of this new chapter, questioning my readiness, my worthiness to take on the role of a father.

As an older first-time father, I came to the table seasoned by life's many trials, triumphs, and tribulations. I had seen enough of life to know its unpredictability, its capacity to surprise and challenge even the most prepared among us. Yet, the thought of cradling my own child, of being responsible for a life so new and fragile, stirred a storm within me. It was as if every excuse, every self-erected barrier was a defense mechanism against the massive changes that were looming on the horizon. The idea of bringing a child into my world brought crashing waves against the shores of my reality, threatening to reshape everything I had known and held dear.

But as the weeks turned into months, something remarkable began to happen. The fears that had once loomed so large began to shrink in the light of new experiences. Each doctor's appointment brought not just news of the baby's growth, but also a deepening connection to the life that was taking shape within Danielle. Each ultrasound, each tiny flutter of a heartbeat that echoed through the speakers, sent a tremor through the walls I had built around my heart. The first kick, a gentle yet unmistakable nudge from beneath the surface of Danielle's growing belly, was more than just a physical sensation. It was a seismic event in the landscape of my soul, shaking loose the doubts and fears that had held me back.

In that electrifying moment, the trepidation that had weighed me down began to dissipate, replaced by a sense of exhilarating anticipation. This wasn't just about becoming a parent; it was about stepping into a new realm of existence, one where love and responsibility intertwined in ways I had never imagined. A child, my child, was reaching out from the unknown, beckoning me to join them on this incredible journey. It was an invitation to become more than I had ever been, to grow alongside this new life as we navigated the world together.

If I could offer any advice to new parents who find themselves standing where I once did, on the precipice of this life-altering voyage, it would be to trust. Trust in the process, trust in the journey, trust in your partner, and above all, trust that parenthood is the most natural thing in the world. There are so many people out there who are far less equipped, less sophisticated, and less wealthy than you, and they've gone on to become outstanding parents. The quality of your own childhood, whether it was filled with love or marred by difficulties, does not determine your success as a parent. What matters most is your willingness to be present, to learn, to grow, and to love unconditionally.

If you or someone you love is about to embark on the journey of parenthood, know this: it is perfectly normal to be terrified. In fact, if you weren't scared, it might mean that you don't care enough. Fear is simply the passion you have for something that you haven't yet conquered. As your baby grows and gains weight, it's not just the child that undergoes a transformation. You, too, will evolve in ways you can't yet fully comprehend. The experience of becoming a parent is one of profound metamorphosis, reshaping not just your life but the very core of who you are.

I am endlessly grateful that I trusted Danielle to bring me along for this wild and wonderful ride. She held my hand and walked with me through the stages of "Will I be a good parent," from denial to acceptance, from disbelief to anticipation, and finally, from excitement to unconditional love. Life has a way of becoming overly complicated with scenarios that run through our minds, with material things that we convince ourselves are essential. But the rhetorical question of "Will I be a good parent?" can be answered with a resounding "Yes" if you simply seek to spend time with your child, to care for them, to laugh with them, and above all, to love them with everything you've got. In the end, being a good parent isn't about perfection. It's about presence, patience, and the willingness to grow alongside your child. It's about understanding that you don't have to have all the answers, you just need to be there, fully and completely. And that, more than anything else, is what makes all the difference.

Good Advice: Thursday Nights

People often advise, "Take one day at a time." It's a simple yet powerful mantra, a piece of wisdom that has guided many through life's toughest moments. But I want to take that advice one step further, offering a slightly unconventional perspective. I suggest you treat every day like it's Thursday night. Now, I know that might sound odd, even a bit specific, but hear me out. There's a method to this Thursday night madness, and it's a mindset that can make navigating life's challenges a little bit easier.

Let's start with the basics: Mondays. Can we all agree that Mondays are, well, the worst? The people who claim to love Mondays are the same people you might expect to see starring in a nightmare-inducing Netflix series one day. Mondays are the Everest of the workweek, standing tall and foreboding after the freedom of the weekend. On the other hand, Fridays, Saturdays, and Sundays are like the sun-drenched valleys, welcomed respites from the daily grind, days that most of us look forward to with eager anticipation.

Taking things one day, or even one hour at a time, is sound advice when you're going through a rough patch. It helps to break down overwhelming tasks into manageable chunks, allowing you to focus on just getting through the next moment. But sometimes, a day or an hour at a time isn't enough of a mental milestone. If you're anything like me, you need something more, a carrot dangling in front of you, motivating you to keep moving forward. And when life doesn't offer that carrot, I've learned to manifest it in my mind.

This is where the Thursday night analogy comes into play. Thursday nights are unique. They hold a special place in the weekly rhythm because they carry the promise of something better just around the corner. Thursday nights are filled with the anticipation of the weekend, a time when you can finally relax, unwind, and enjoy the fruits of your labor. The workweek is nearly over, and there's a sense of accomplishment in making it this far. You might still have one more day to push through, but you do so with the knowledge that a break, a reward, is imminent.

I recommend adopting this Thursday night mindset as you navigate life's challenges. Imagine that you just need to get through one more day, one more workday, one more difficult conversation, one more stretch of stress, and then you'll reach your "weekend," whatever that might represent for you. Break it down even further if necessary: just three more appointments, 42 more emails, two more meetings, and then something significantly better awaits you on the other side. This mindset has helped me immensely during rough times. I remind myself that I just need to power through nine more hours, and then I'll be home to my loved ones, my coping tools, and the things that bring me comfort and joy.

For me, those tools include our pets, journaling, passion projects, sports, faith, meditation, and gym time. All of these activities are part of my personal "weekend," the time when I can recharge and find relief from the stresses of life. In my mind, these healing and distracting activities are just around the corner, waiting for me at the end of the day. By embracing this Thursday night mindset, even the most dreaded, awful Monday can be faced with a sense of hope and anticipation. Dangle that carrot of hope in front of yourself to get through your worst days, and before you know it, Thursday night will be here, bringing with it the promise of something better.

Remember, life is full of ups and downs, and the tough days can feel like they'll never end. But by breaking down the week into manageable pieces and looking forward to the "weekend" that awaits, you can find the strength to keep going. Treat every day like it's Thursday night, and you'll find that the challenges you face are a little easier to bear. So go ahead, dangle that carrot, and keep moving forward. The weekend is closer than you think.

CHAPTER 3

Time Stood Still

After months of anticipation, we finally received the phone call we had been eagerly waiting for, a room was available at the local hospital in Bakersfield, CA. It was around 4 a.m. on January 5th, 2023, long before the sun had begun its ascent. We were buzzing with excitement, feeling ready for the moment that would change our lives forever. The bags had been packed for days, the car seat inspected and secured, and the nameplate and first photo outfit for our daughter, Violet, carefully chosen. My picture-perfect, pregnant bride stepped into the car, and we drove the familiar route to the hospital, a drive I had rehearsed countless times, preparing for this very day.

Upon arrival, we were shown to our room, the space where we would meet Violet for the first time. Danielle settled onto the twin bed that would soon become the center of our world. As I paced the room, alternating between sitting on the most uncomfortable couch I had ever encountered and standing by Danielle's side, we both tried to remain patient. Her process of dilation was slow, and hours stretched into another day. We shared food, laughs, and the kind of intimate moments that only come when you're waiting for something extraordinary. We joked about the "burrito from hell" that had my stomach in knots, adding a layer of discomfort to an already tense situation. The hours blurred together, and as January 5th became January 6th, our patience began to wane. The evening dragged on, and Danielle was still only dilated by a centimeter or two.

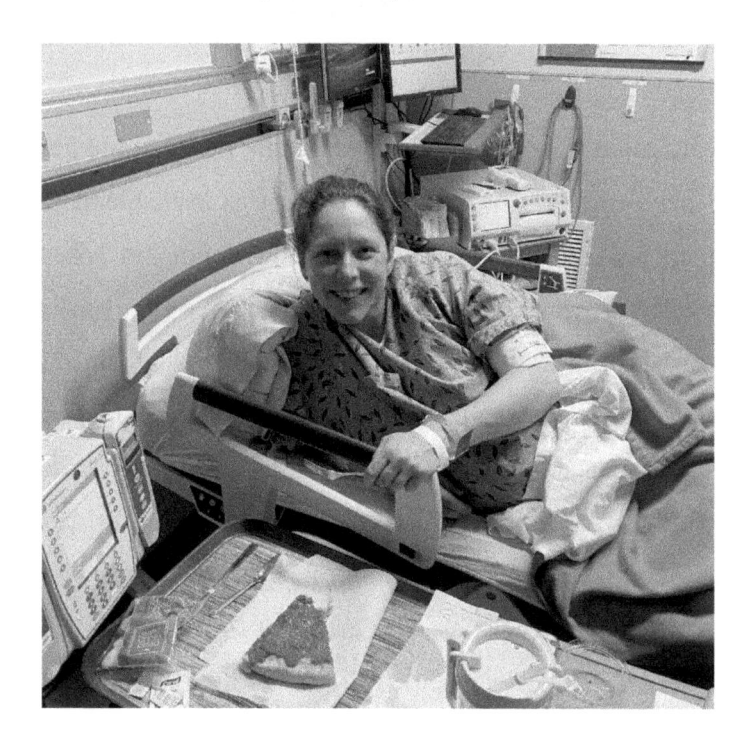

Throughout this time, the heart monitor attached to Danielle's belly provided a constant, reassuring rhythm, a reminder that Violet was there, waiting to join us. The steady beat became a kind of lullaby, a soothing sound despite its intrusion on our attempts to rest. But then, around 8 p.m. that evening, the pace of the monitor's cadence slowed, and Danielle sprung up abruptly. She alerted me, and I deflected, telling her in jest that she was being too much of an ICU nurse. Within

30 seconds, the hospital staff team rushed in. Chaos ensued as blood had poured from my girls, pooling in the bed. There was blood all over Danielle, and the bed. There was so much blood, staining the bed, her clothes, and our hopes for a smooth delivery. As the nurses rushed in, their faces did not mask their concentration and urgency of the situation. They barked orders as Danielle, moving with a speed I hadn't seen in weeks, twisted and turned into various positions at their command. Just minutes before, she had been moving at a crawl, her body heavy with the burden of impending motherhood. Now, driven by pure terror, she was nimble, focused solely on protecting our daughter. In the blink of an eye, my best friend, my wife, my everything, was whisked away for an emergency c-section, her life and our daughter's hanging in the balance.

"I love you," I yelled after her, my voice cracking with fear. Her terrified cries echoed back, pleading with the medical team, "Please save my baby." Then she was gone, leaving me alone in a sterile room that had, in an instant, transformed from a place of joyful expectation to a chamber of dread. I collapsed to my knees, tears streaming down my face, and prayed harder than I ever had before. In those moments, I had never felt so vulnerable, so utterly alone. My mind raced with images of the worst-case scenario, my heart barely able to withstand the fear. Minutes felt like hours as I paced the hallway, desperate for answers. I walked up and down the corridors, searching for any sign of life, any indication of what was happening to my girls. But the hallway was empty, eerily silent, as if the entire hospital held its breath, waiting for the outcome. I returned to the room, picked up my phone, and began calling family and close friends, needing to hear a familiar voice, to feel some connection to the outside world as our lives spiraled into the unimaginable.

I sat alone in that room for what felt like an eternity, each second dragging on with excruciating slowness. My thoughts were a chaotic whirlpool of fear, hope, and despair. How were my girls? Is Danielle okay? Will Violet survive? It was as if I had been thrust into a twisted Netflix drama, only this was no fiction, this was our life, unraveling before my eyes. As the minutes ticked by, stretching into 50 of the longest damn minutes of my life, I prepared myself for the worst. The door finally opened, and a somber-faced staff member motioned for me to follow. With each step, my heart pounded louder in my chest, the weight of impending doom pressing down on me.

As I entered the operating area, the gravity of the situation hit me like a freight train. The staff's expressions were grim, their body language heavy with the burden of what they had just witnessed. I could hear the cries of newborns in the distance, but the only sound I strained to hear was that of my own family. Then, like a beacon in the fog, I heard Danielle's voice, weak but insistent, "Where is my baby?" In that moment, I was simultaneously crushed and grateful, grateful that Danielle was alive, but crushed by the knowledge that something was terribly wrong.

I approached Danielle's bedside, trying to be strong for her as she sobbed, "Where is my baby?" My gut churned with dread, but I forced myself to remain hopeful, to hold on to the sliver of possibility that Violet might be okay. The doctor approached us, her face a mask of sorrow, and I knew before she spoke that our worst fears were about to be confirmed. She explained that Violet was in critical condition, having endured 16 minutes of CPR and chest compressions just to keep her alive. Her words were a blur, fragments of horror that I could barely process. I only caught about every 5th word. "Breathing tube... machines... sustain life..." My mind couldn't fully absorb the reality of what she was saying. It was as if I were watching from a distance, detached from my own life, unable to grasp the magnitude of our loss.

When I finally saw Violet in the ICU, surrounded by machines that beeped and whirred in a symphony of despair, my heart shattered. There she was, our little girl, a fragile life tethered to technology, her tiny body fighting a battle she never had a chance to win. No amount of medical intervention could disguise the stark truth that we were facing, the truth that we were about to lose our daughter. Danielle and I, united in love and grief, could do nothing but hold hands and weep silently, our hearts breaking with every passing second.

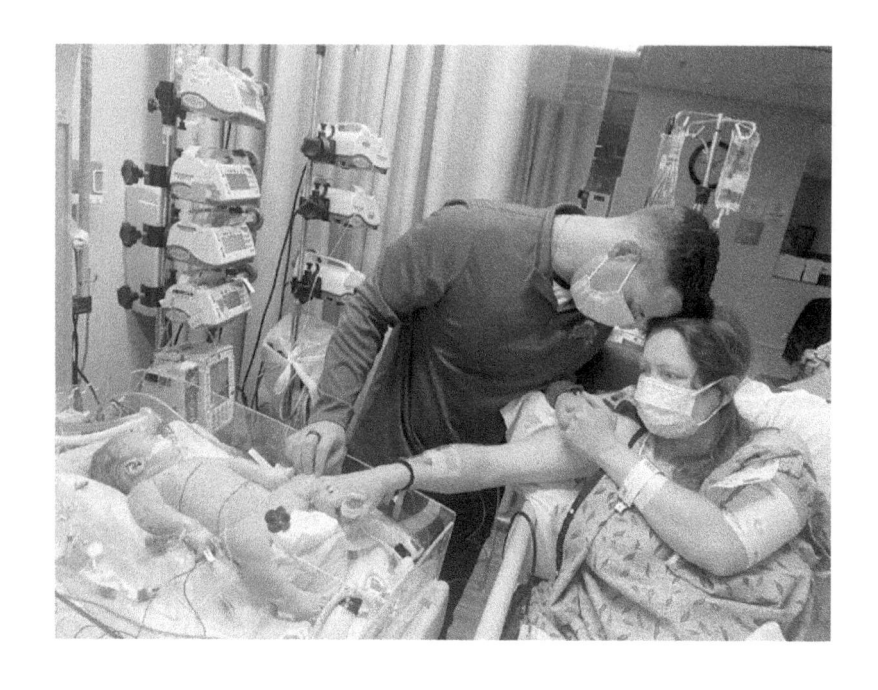

Violet had lost so much blood during the c-section, and now she depended on machines to sustain her life. With Danielle's medical background, relationships, and fantastic advocacy partners, we were fortunate to gain insights and second opinions from some of the brightest medical minds in the United States. We connected the fantastic local medical director with some leading medical staff from the southeast U.S. We advocated hard for our little girl, but unfortunately, the updates were not improving, and all of our trusted colleagues ultimately agreed with the local medical leaders. The prognosis remained grim. The updates were a devastating repetition of the same tragic news, Violet would not survive without the machines. We were faced with an impossible decision: how long do we keep Vio on life support, knowing that she will never breathe on her own?

The weight of that decision crushed us, but we knew we had to let her go. We couldn't bear the thought of prolonging her suffering. In our lowest moment, we sought comfort from a few faith leader friends. We wanted Violet to be baptized before she met God. Although it was the middle of the night, the hospital was able to help us. Despite the late hour, a pastor arrived, and in a moment that was both heart-wrenching and beautiful, Violet was baptized. We sobbed uncontrollably as we made the impossible decision to remove her from life support.

In the "grieving suite" at the end of the hall, marked by a butterfly logo that silently communicated our loss to the staff, we held Violet in our arms for the first and last time. Without the machines to keep her alive, we watched as her life slipped away. Her tiny body grew cold and stiff in our arms, her spirit fluttering away like the butterfly on the door. We spent those last hours with her, holding her, singing to her, memorizing every delicate feature of her face. We cried until there were no tears left, and then we cried some more.

The hospital provided us with a "baby chiller" so that we could keep Violet's body cool and spend a few more precious hours with her. It was a morbid and surreal experience, but it allowed us to take photos with her, photos that we now treasure more than anything. They are the only tangible memories we have of our daughter, the only proof that she was here, that she is ours. Violet, our beautiful, innocent daughter, never got to take a breath on her own. She never got to cry, or laugh, or smile. She never got to grow up, to experience the world, to fulfill the potential that she held within her tiny body. The pain of that loss is something I carry with me every day. It's a weight that never truly goes away, a reminder of what could have been.

In those final moments, as we held Violet's lifeless body, I found a flicker of hope in the fact that Danielle had survived. My wife, my rock, my partner in this journey of healing, was still with me. We were united in our sorrow, bound by a loss that words could never fully express. And as we said goodbye to Violet, as the medical staff wheeled her away from us, we found some small comfort in knowing that she was no longer in pain. We were left with only each other and the overwhelming task of finding a way to move forward.

That night, I crawled into the small twin bed at the hospital with Danielle, and I held her as she cried herself to sleep. There was nothing left to say, no words that could make sense of what we had just experienced. We were completely devastated, our world shattered, but we were still together. And in that togetherness, I found the strength to face another day, to take one small step forward, even as the ground beneath us crumbled.

Coping Tools - Faith

Faith is not something I've often talked about openly. My experiences with faith as a child were tumultuous at best, leaving me with a complicated relationship with belief. It wasn't until about five years ago that I was baptized, a decision that came after much reflection and soul-searching. As a local government leader, I've also been conditioned to keep faith and work separate, a principle ingrained in me through years of service. Mixing church and state was not just frowned upon but actively discouraged in several of my past organizations. So, writing this subsection does make me a little uneasy. Yet, the past two years have tested our faith in ways that cannot be ignored, compelling me to confront these feelings head-on.

When you hold your perfect newborn daughter's lifeless body in your arms, when you drive home from the hospital with an empty car seat, when you walk into a nursery that will never hear her cries, it shatters something deep within you. It has a way of making you angry at God, at the universe, at anything that could have the power to prevent such an unfathomable loss. We didn't just doubt God; we were irate with Him. It felt as though everything we believed in, everything we had faith in, had betrayed us in the cruelest way possible. These emotions were a part of my early stages of grief, a natural response to the seemingly unjust twists of fate that left us broken.

As the days of anguish turned into weeks and months, I noticed something shifting within us. At first, it was subtle, almost unnoticeable. But as the anger ebbed and flowed, something else began to take root. We started to see that God was working, not through grand gestures or miraculous signs, but through the people around us. The kindness, the prayers, the unwavering support of our neighbors, our community, our friends, and our family. They began to chip away at the icy walls we had built around our hearts, slowly eroding the massive chip on our shoulders. It was as though God was reaching out to us through them, offering solace in the only way we could accept at that moment.

Ironically, we found ourselves more connected to our church and its faith leaders after Violet's passing than ever before. The same church that hosted her services, a place we once attended out of routine, became a sanctuary for our wounded souls. Our church, aptly named The Bridge, served as just that, a bridge over the perilous chasm of fury and uncertainty that threatened to swallow us whole. We were inching our way through the stages of grief, and while we were far from healed, moving from rock bottom to simply being deeply hurt was, in its own way, major progress.

Our deepening faith has continued to be a source of comfort when earthly remedies alone cannot console us. There's something instinctive about turning to God in times of crisis, especially when medicine and technology, in all their advancements, fail to right the wrongs that life throws at us. Over the last year, our regular attendance at church has evolved from a weekly routine into an integral part of our lives. It's no longer just about the sermons or the rituals; it's about the people, the sense of community, and the shared experience of navigating life's trials together.

The pastoral team, recognizing our journey, extended their care far beyond formalities. They became a source of comfort and guidance, their words and actions steeped in genuine concern for our well-being. Staying after services for discussions, for fellowship, deepened our sense of belonging. We weren't just attendees; we were seen, cared for, and embraced as part of a larger community. It was a feeling that was both healing and empowering, a reminder that we were not alone in our suffering. Through these experiences, I've come to understand the multifaceted role of faith in coping with grief. It's not merely about religious teachings or rituals; it's about the human connections forged within a faith community. It's about being part of a collective journey, where support is given and received, where stories of loss and hope intertwine, creating a tapestry of shared experience that can be both comforting and enlightening.

We aren't the type of people to force our views on faith, nor are we the types to let our faith remain dormant until the turbulence of life awakens a primal yearning for support beyond the tangible. But in the months since our great loss, we've noticed that the small wins, the moments of peace and clarity, have continued to pile up. Some might chalk this up to luck, to the universe finding a balance after one of life's biggest setbacks. But we prefer to see it as faith. Faith that healing is possible, faith that the power of prayer can manifest in our lives in ways we never anticipated.

People often use the phrase "let go and let God." It's one of those sayings that can sound cliché, almost trite, until you're in the midst of a storm and have no other choice but to let go. As the waves and cycles of grief crash into the shores of your sanity, the best advice I can offer from a faith perspective is to give your problems, your sorrow, your grief, and your anger to God. Turn it all over to Him, and you will feel the weight of your tragedy lifted in due time. In His time.

This journey through faith and grief has not been easy, nor has it been straightforward. It's been a winding road, full of unexpected turns and steep climbs. But through it all, we've found that faith isn't about having all the answers; it's about trusting the process, about believing that even in the darkest moments, there is a light that can guide you forward. Sometimes, that light comes not from above, but from the people around you, the community that holds you up when you can't stand on your own. In these moments, I've learned that faith isn't just a belief, it's a lifeline, a connection to something greater than ourselves, something that gives us the strength to keep going, even when we feel like we can't take another step.

Journal Journey – January 10, 2023 (the week of her passing)

In these traumatic moments, time didn't just stand still; it twisted and contorted into something unrecognizable. Everything we knew collapsed as we faced the devastating loss of Violet, our precious first-born child. The universe felt like it had paused, trapping us in a nightmare where past, present, and future merged into a single, unbearable reality. Outside, the world kept moving, oblivious to our shattered lives. For us, nothing would ever be the same again.

In those first hours, surrounded by a blur of white coats and the relentless beeping of machines, Danielle and I clung to each other with a desperation I had never known. Our dreams lay in pieces around us, but our love remained, the only thing untouched by the devastation. We held on tight, grasping for any semblance of stability as everything else crumbled away. Almost without realizing it, we found ourselves reaching out for something beyond us, something that could possibly carry the weight of our overwhelming sorrow.

Faith had never been my go-to in times of trouble. It was always there, lingering quietly in the background as we built our hopeful lives together. We acknowledged it occasionally, offering a nod during moments of gratitude or fleeting fear, but it was never something we leaned on heavily. After Violet's death, that changed. Standing on the edge of an abyss filled with despair, faith surged forward, demanding to be felt and acknowledged in a way I had never experienced before. This turn toward faith wasn't planned or even fully conscious. It was raw and instinctual, a primal urge to find meaning in the midst of senseless tragedy. I had heard people say that faith is a refuge for the weary heart, a lifeline when you're drowning in loss. Now, submerged in those turbulent waters, I understood that sentiment with painful clarity.

My prayers during that time were anything but polished. They were messy, broken fragments of words spilling out between sobs. I begged, questioned, and raged at God, unfiltered and unrestrained. There was no hiding the anger and confusion that tore through me. Yet, amidst the turmoil, there was also a desperate plea for strength, for some way to survive the unbearable pain that had taken hold of our lives. Faith didn't offer answers or immediate comfort. It didn't erase the hurt or map out a path through the darkness. What it did provide was a space to unload the crushing weight that pressed down on our hearts. It allowed us to acknowledge our vulnerability openly, without shame or reservation. In the quiet moments of prayer, whether voiced aloud or whispered in our minds, we found a shared language of grief and a flicker of hope that we so desperately needed.

As Danielle and I prayed together, sometimes sitting in silence and other times through tears, a fragile sense of comfort began to emerge. Letting go of the need to understand why this had happened brought a small measure of relief. Trusting that we didn't have to carry this burden alone, that something greater than us was present in our suffering, offered a sliver of solace amid the chaos. Faith became a vital link between us and God, but also between each other. It opened doors for deeper vulnerability, allowing us to share our darkest fears and deepest sorrows without fear of judgment. We mourned together, held each other through the waves of pain, and found tiny sparks of hope in simply being present for one another. In the days following Violet's death, we realized that faith wasn't about having answers. It was about trusting that somehow, even in the darkest times, we could keep moving forward.

Faith didn't change what happened. Violet was still gone, and our hearts were still broken. But it changed something within us. It softened some of the sharpest edges of our grief and gave us the strength to take one step, then another, even when the path ahead was shrouded in darkness. In surrendering to the uncertainty and embracing faith, we found a fragile, new kind of peace. It wasn't about understanding or accepting the loss, but about trusting that, somehow, we would find our way through the pain together.

Lessons Learned – Give Grace

When your world is turned upside down to the point where you no longer recognize the life you once knew, you will find yourself riding a relentless tide of emotions. These emotions don't adhere to a schedule or a predictable pattern. They come in waves, sometimes gently lapping at the shore, offering a momentary respite, and other times crashing down like a tsunami, overwhelming you all at once. In those initial stages, you have no control over these feelings. They arrive uninvited and leave just as abruptly, often leaving you breathless in their wake.

As you navigate this emotional turmoil, you will also notice the impact it has on those closest to you. Your family, your friends, even empathetic acquaintances, many of them will grieve heavily alongside you, their hearts breaking as they try to share in your pain. Here is the thing that nobody really talks about: grief is a deeply personal experience. It's a journey that, while shared with others, is also intensely solitary. In that solitude, you'll start to see things differently.

Selfishly speaking, one of the most painful revelations in this process is realizing that some of your "closest friends" may not be the ones who are there for you when your heart is sliced in two. When Violet passed, it was hard for us not to notice who was present in our lives and who wasn't. There's a certain expectation, perhaps unrealistic, that those who know us best will be the first to step up, to offer comfort, to stand by our side. When they don't, it feels like another blow, another wound on top of the one you're already struggling to heal. It's not something you want to dwell on, but it's there, gnawing at the edges of your grief.

The absence of certain people during such a pivotal moment was glaring. I hate even thinking about these things, much less typing them to print. But the truth is, it was a real challenge for us. We learned along the way that our family, friends, coworkers, and neighbors simply didn't know how to grieve for and with us. It's a harsh reality, but one worth acknowledging. Some of our long-time friends disappeared for a while after Violet's passing, not because they didn't care, but because they felt so awful and had no idea what to say or do to comfort and console us. They were lost in their own uncertainty, paralyzed by the fear of saying or doing the wrong thing.

Conversely, we were surprised by the people who did show up, those we had only known for a few months, who turned into some of our greatest sources of strength. They became our guardian angels, fast friends who stepped in and held us up when we could barely stand. Danielle and I often say that despite being new to our community during our loss, we are so grateful that we were in Bakersfield, CA, when tragedy struck. The support, empathy, and outpouring of love we received from people who had known us for such a short time was nothing short of miraculous. For weeks, homemade food appeared at our doorstep, contributions poured in to help with hospital bills, and we received copious amounts of thoughtful cards and gifts. These gestures were not just acts of kindness; they were lifelines, pulling us back from the brink.

We developed true lifelong friendships out of this tragedy. We forged bonds in the fires of grief that will never be broken. It's hard to imagine how we would have survived those early days without our community. The strength of a community, we learned, is essential to the healing process. And we were blessed to find ourselves in the midst of an amazing one.

Here is another truth: everyone handles stress, hardships, grief, and death differently. We had to learn to acknowledge that everyone has their own limitations in expressing sympathy. Just because someone doesn't react the way you want or expect them to doesn't mean they care any less. People are not lesser friends if they don't show up the way you imagined they would. This isn't high school, where every slight feels like a personal affront. In times of deep grief, it's essential to allow people the space to find their own way to express their condolences or support. Everyone's process is different, and that's okay.

Recognize their intentions, even when their attempts to console might not be perfect. Appreciate the effort, the thought behind the action, rather than focusing on how it falls short of your expectations. When someone inadvertently causes pain with their words or actions, try to forgive their missteps. It's not easy, especially when you're already hurting, but it's necessary for your own peace of mind. Try to see things from their perspective, understanding that they, too, may feel helpless in the face of your loss.

It's not fair to yourself or to your friends and family to gauge their value based on how they respond to your grief. I know this sounds strange, considering we were the ones reeling, but for the sake of our own mental well-being, we realized that we had to reset and eliminate all expectations for our circle. We had to give everyone around us a lot of grace. Even the most empathetic people don't always know what to say or do. By giving others grace, you are setting a standard for yourself as well.

When you are totally overwhelmed with sadness and anger, you will need to give yourself a lot of space to heal, mourn, and grieve. In the moment, this is much easier said than done. You will need to have an accountability partner or team to assist and remind you. These are the people who will ask the simple questions that can make a big difference: Did you eat today? Have you showered in the last few days? Little things like brushing your teeth, flossing, putting on lotion, and shaving go a long way toward feeling a little better about yourself. In the middle of your healing journey, you aren't thinking about yourself; you are consumed by your pain. This is where your circle can support you the most. So, as you navigate the choppy waters of grief, remember to give grace, to others and to yourself. Allow yourself the space to heal at your own pace, without judgment or expectation. And know that it's okay to lean on your community, even when they don't always get it right. They're doing their best, just like you are. In the end, that's all any of us can do.

Good Advice – Allow Yourself to Feel

In the aftermath of losing a child, the world can feel like a cold, unrecognizable place. It's a reality no parent ever wants to face, and when it comes crashing down, it's overwhelming in ways words can scarcely convey. The pain is not just deep; it's all-encompassing, touching every aspect of your life, every breath you take, every thought that crosses your mind. In these moments, advice can feel distant, hollow, or even irrelevant. I contemplated not sharing good advice for this chapter, as it is in immediately following loss. I went back and forth and then landed on one piece of guidance that may offer some small relief: Allow yourself to feel.

This isn't about simply sitting with your pain, though that's part of it. It's about giving yourself permission to experience the full spectrum of your emotions, anger, sorrow, confusion, and even moments of numbness. Grief is not a linear process, nor is it predictable. There will be days when the tears come unexpectedly, triggered by something as simple as a song on the radio, a passing comment, or something that occurs in a show you are watching. There will be days when the pain is so intense it feels like a physical weight pressing down on you, and there will be days when you feel nothing at all, and that emptiness can be just as terrifying.

Allowing yourself to feel means recognizing that there is no "right" way to grieve. Society often imposes unspoken timelines or expectations on how we should handle loss, urging us to be strong, to move on, to find closure. These notions can feel cruelly out of sync with the reality of what you're experiencing. The truth is, you may never "move on" from this kind of loss, and that's okay. What matters is that you move forward in whatever way makes sense for you, and that begins with honoring your feelings. This advice is about embracing vulnerability. It's about understanding that your grief is a reflection of your love, and there is no shame in feeling deeply. In fact, it's through allowing yourself to fully experience these emotions that you begin to find a path toward healing. It's not about rushing the process or forcing yourself to be "okay" when you're not. It's about giving yourself the grace to grieve in your own time and in your own way.

Allowing yourself to feel also means accepting the moments of relief or joy when they come, without guilt. Grief doesn't mean you're doomed to a life devoid of happiness. There will be moments, however fleeting, when you laugh, when you feel a glimmer of hope or peace. Allow yourself to feel those moments too, without the burden of thinking that they somehow diminish your grief or the memory of your child. These moments are not a betrayal; they are part of the complexity of the human experience. No matter what I am feeling inside, I always makes efforts to be silly to get Danielle to laugh.

In allowing yourself to feel, you are not just enduring the storm, you are engaging with it, understanding its power, and recognizing that within the tempest of grief, there are lessons about love, resilience, and the strength of the human spirit. By embracing all of your emotions, you honor the depth of your loss and the significance of your love. In a world that often encourages us to hide our pain, to put on a brave face, this chapter serves as a gentle reminder that true courage lies in vulnerability. It's okay to break down, to cry, to be angry, and to be lost. It's okay to not have all the answers. And most importantly, it's okay to allow yourself to feel, fully and without apology. It's through this process that you begin to heal, not by erasing the pain, but by integrating it into your life in a way that allows you to carry it with strength, with love, and with the knowledge that your feelings, no matter how intense, are valid and necessary.

CHAPTER 4
Shock and Denial

We would ultimately learn that Violet and Danielle had an undiagnosed case of vasa previa. In basic terms, an extra vessel grew on the outside of the placenta. The vessel ruptured while we were in the process of her dilating for birth. All of the blood that poured out of Danielle was ultimately Violet's blood. The reality of that moment still haunts me. In a way, Violet saved Danielle's life. I still have the blood-stained shirt from that day. It's not something I can bring myself to part with, nor would I want to. That stain is more than just a mark, it's a tangible reminder of the most excruciating day of my life, a day that altered the course of our existence. I don't think I will ever try to have the stain removed. Danielle and I had to stay at the hospital for a few days after Violet passed as she recovered from what proved to be a life-and-death situation. It seemed statistically impossible that we would come home without Violet. However, we learned that the rare version of vasa previa that we encountered only occurs about 1 in 35,000 to 1 in 50,000 times during birth.

We were reeling, and nothing felt real. The world outside the hospital windows moved forward, but for us, time had stopped. I didn't think it was possible to feel everything and nothing all at once until we left the hospital together and walked out to an empty car seat. The surrealness of that moment still sends shivers down my spine. It's an image I replay over and over in my mind, the car seat that was supposed to carry our daughter home, now a stark emblem of loss. I knew I had to hold it together for Danielle on the drive home, so I didn't even look in the back seat. It felt as if acknowledging that empty seat would make the pain unbearable, as though it would break the fragile hold I had on my emotions. We shared the news with a few close friends while at the hospital, then a few days later via social media. The words felt hollow, insufficient, but they were all we had.

We awoke the next day to the silence of an empty nursery, a meticulously crafted haven of hope and dreams now echoing with the hollowness of absence. The floral wallpaper that Danielle put up herself during a 2 a.m. "nesting session" still loomed large, its vibrant colors now a painful reminder of the life that was meant to fill this space. The floral blooms, a bittersweet tapestry where each petal whispers "Violet," her name an agonizing fixture upon the wall, as though the very room breathes a life its occupant never got to. This nursery, once a vessel of anticipation, now sails a sea of sorrow, in an ocean full of what-could-have-beens. Every detail speaks of preparation made with love, the crib with its uncreased sheets patterned with the playful safari theme we envisioned, the tiny clothes folded neatly in drawers, waiting to be worn. The crib stands ready, a silent sentinel guarding the empty space where Violet should be. The untouched tranquility of the room is a stark testament to the turmoil within, a visual metaphor for the anger and denial that courses through a bereaved parent's heart.

To pass by this room was to navigate a corridor of grief. I instinctively avoided the entire hallway, each step towards it laden with a heartache too immense to face. This was not just an empty room; it was an emblem of loss, a space where every corner is filled with the gravity of a life's promise unfulfilled. The door remained closed, a barrier between the unbearable reality inside and the fragile world we tried to piece together outside. Here, in the silence, the shadows of anger and denial dance together, dark partners in the intricate ballet of mourning. It is simultaneously a haunted and sacred space, paying homage to the profound depth of sorrow that seeks solace in the remembrance of a daughter deeply loved, profoundly missed, and forever cherished. In the stillness of the nursery, where the light plays upon the walls adorned with blooms and butterflies, there lies a heartbreaking void. It's a space perfectly poised for the symphony of life, a symphony that remains hauntingly unfinished.

The name 'Violet' adorns the floral wall above the crib. Her name, once danced on the tongues of expectant parents, now a sacred whisper, a testament to absence. The crib, with its slats never warmed by tiny grasps, its mattress never molded by the gentle heft of a newborn, stands as a silent sentry to the stark reality of a dream unfulfilled. My avoidance of this corridor, a natural reflex, is not merely a path untaken but a march into the flurry of denial and pain. Here, within these four walls, the air is thick with the weight of an anger that burns silently, a searing reminder of a future stolen, a narrative abruptly halted, an existence deeply yearned for yet never realized. This emptiness is not a simple absence of presence; it is a presence in itself, a palpable, overwhelming force that fills each corner with the dense gravity of loss. To enter this room is to confront the unspoken, to face the profound anguish of love that has no physical form to nurture, a care with no focal point of affection. I was not ready for that yet.

Family, friends, neighbors, colleagues, and our communities became our lifeline, serving in the invaluable role as our recovery team, following our tragedy. The communal grief that others shared with us served as a powerful reminder to us of the collective human experience. The compassion of others still amazes us, and the strength that can be found even in our most vulnerable moments. Our story is a testament to survival amidst the unthinkable. We hope that our openness and experience can be a beacon for others navigating their own dark waters. We were tested in ways we never imagined, and our reflections since can hopefully provide an important dimension for someone in need of answers or inspiration.

The path forward was not one of healing in a straight line, but rather a winding road with countless detours and dead ends. It was through the love and support of our community that we were able to begin the process of stitching our lives back together, piece by painful piece. Each gesture of kindness, each word of sympathy, was like a small patch on the quilt of our shattered existence. They didn't fix the tear, but they helped hold it together. As we moved through those early days, we learned that while the pain would never fully dissipate, it could be woven into the fabric of our lives in a way that honored Violet's memory. This journey of grief and healing is one that will continue for the rest of our lives, but we are not walking it alone. We are surrounded by a network of love and support that reminds us, even on the darkest days, that we are not defined by our loss, but by the love we carry with us.

Coping Tools – Pets

Pets are the absolute best when you don't feel like being around anyone other than your significant other. If you don't feel like talking, or even showering, the only people who won't care and still can't wait to be close are your pets. Up until late 2023, we had three cats and one dog. To say they are a part of the family is an epic understatement. With all due respect to our good friends, there is no one else we would rather be around than Cole, Murphy, and Stella…RIP Simon. Obviously, my wife is included; I am a little smarter than I look. These furry family members truly are our service animals. I know they always have been, but it became even more apparent to me after Violet passed. Our pets are magical little empaths that yearn for nothing more than to hear "good boy/girl." They soak away the negativity and thaw the depression we often sit with.

In the landscape of our grief, where human words often fall short, the silent support of our cherished pets has been a balm to our aching hearts. To say they are a part of the family barely scratches the surface of their significance in our lives. Their presence has been a constant source of comfort, their intuitive empathy a gift beyond measure. In their simple acts of curling up beside us, offering a nudge of a nose, or the soft purr of contentment, they bring a sense of peace that is hard to find elsewhere. Our pets, in their unassuming way, have the power to absorb the heavy air of sorrow and replace it with something lighter. They don't ask for much, a positive affirmation, a gentle pat, or a moment of play. They give us so much in return. In their eyes, we find unconditional love, in their companionship, a quiet strength.

My therapist had conditioned me and cautioned me about the importance of not avoiding my feelings. I was also advised to let myself feel everything and to acknowledge the pain as part of my healing process. As elementary as it may sound, before I was able to share a lot of my anger, despair, or sadness with others, I talked to my pets about it. God had heard it, of course, but I didn't want to risk upsetting my wife or close friends. The last thing a close friend wants to hear every week is their buddy ugly crying. So, I would vent to the furry fam. They heard it all, rage, depression, denial, doubt, and eventually the comeback. Saying all of it out loud helped me to process my grief and anger, until enough time passed that Danielle and I could talk about certain subjects together.

Reflecting on the role of pets in my life, I've come to understand more deeply how animals can alleviate a lot of gloom and turn it to joy. They are attuned to our emotions, always ready to offer their presence as a refuge from the storms of sadness. They soak up the negativity, thaw the frost of depression, and remind us of the uncomplicated joys of life. The best support doesn't come from words or grand gestures, but from the simple, steadfast presence of those who ask for nothing but offer everything. For anyone walking through the valley of grief, I recommend finding solace in the company of pets. Whether they are cats, dogs, or any other animal, their ability to heal, to understand without speaking, and to be present in our moments of need is a form of therapy that often goes unspoken but is felt deeply in the heart.

Journal Journey – February 25, 2023

It has been nearly two months since Violet left this world. In some ways, it feels like it was yesterday, and in others, like it was a lifetime ago. Danielle and I are bickering more frequently over dumb little stuff than we have in the past. We both often realize and apologize to each other as it occurs. We are on edge. The irony is that I would never condone anyone else being so snippy with her. It makes me sad to reflect on this. I reflect the most when she is away from the house, for better and worse. I realize how far I still have to go, grow, and heal. After nearly losing Danielle, along with Violet, I worry about her constantly when she is not with me. I worry about her safety, well-being, and how she is doing mentally. She is my everything. My therapist says that this isn't something to be embarrassed about. Saying that it is a part of my grieving process, and everyone's process is unique to their experiences and emotions.

Danielle had only been away from the house for about 90 minutes. Yet, I have looked to see what time it is, or if I have missed a call, at least a dozen times. The walls echo with the sharpness of memories. Here, in the silence, I am left with the shadow of January 7th. It is a day that carved a chasm in my world. It is in these quiet spaces that the absence is most palpable, where the mind wanders through the corridors of 'what if' and 'if only.' Counselors have offered tools, friends have given their time, and yet, solitude remains my most challenging opponent. I've found the most relief in the presence of my beloved Danielle; her absence amplifies the emptiness left by Violet. I joke that I'm a little crazy with her but a lot crazier without her. It's a line tossed with a laugh in public, but it's rooted in the stark truth of my private reality. A case of sarcasm being used to keep others from feeling awkward from the joke.

I am known to be a very optimistic person and have worked hard to develop that skill set. However, I feel as though I am going to have to rebuild every part of my life. I know I need to take everything a day at a time, but that is so much easier said than done. Sometimes the bravest face we show is to ourselves in the mirror. It's an acknowledgment that strength is not in the absence of fear, but with the courage to voice it. It feels as though the world has moved on around us, while we are standing still in a state of shock. I know I am supposed to miss my wife when she is gone, but this is just silly. I simply don't feel like me without her.

Lessons Learned – Working Through the Pain

I am a little ashamed to admit this, but I was the kid that flipped the Monopoly board if it looked like I wasn't going to come out on top. I hate losing and not being good at things so much. I have always been extremely competitive. I want to be the best at all that I do. Sometimes it becomes an obstacle for me because I struggle to get through the initial growing pains of not being good at something before I could have turned the corner into being great at it. I am always looking to grow and seek to align myself with leading organizations, institutions, mentors, and colleagues. If you asked me two years ago, I would have told you that the formula for success is mildly straightforward: work hard, treat people with kindness, and follow nationwide best practices.

When tragedy strikes and your first-born child dies, all that goes out the window. Instantly you are swept up into emotions you never imagined you could have. I shut down. I didn't even want to talk on the phone to some of my best friends. I struggled to get out of bed in the morning, to eat, to brush my hair, and to see past the trauma looming over us. One of the biggest challenges was that when Violet passed away, I was only six months into my new role. I was just getting up to speed and feeling good about how my teams and I were doing. Unfortunately, I was still relatively new and had not accumulated much sick or vacation time yet. Danielle was not working full-time, so I had to put on my smile-adorned mask and get back to the office.

I received a great deal of grace early on, and expectations were certainly lowered for me upon my return. I would be lying if I told you that I was anywhere close to my former self. In some ways, I am not sure if I ever will be that person again. I felt as though my previous strength as a multi-tasker was gone, along with my ability to focus. I thrive on being a high-energy, relationship-driven connector and cheerleader. I would only get visits from that guy about twice a week. It was twice as challenging to play that role for a while. Consistency has been a major challenge the past year, even with me committing to therapy and many other strategic coping tools. It is not a good look when the cheerleader is the one that needs to be rallied. I cannot tell you how upset it makes me as a driven, alpha type, to know that I did not get to showcase the best version of me on a regular basis in Bakersfield.

I am blessed to have a career and a leader in my organization that has not just provided flexibility but truly empathized with my family. I cannot say enough wonderful things about my supervisor and City Manager, Christian Clegg. He is the real deal, and I can only hope that you get to work with someone like him one day. He has come over to my house to drop off food for us on Thanksgiving. He spoke at Violet's celebration of life ceremony. He and his wife regularly would check in on Danielle and I during our attempt to find normalcy again in 2023 and beyond. He and my amazing peer took on so many things for me during my grace period in the office. I don't know if, or how we would have bounced back had we been in a different environment.

An important lesson that I learned in the past two years was to not share too much with too many people. This was a powerful lesson in discernment, in recognizing the boundaries we had to draw, not out of cynicism, but self-preservation. We learned to embrace the solace found in solitude and the select company of those who offered genuine support. In those delicate times, we came to understand the intricate dance between vulnerability and strength. It's not about building walls but rather fortifying our hearts. As we heal and move forward, we carry with us a refined sense of who we are and who we can count on.

We are now more attuned to the intentions of others, filtering out noise and nurturing only those bonds that are sincere. The road to recovery is one we walk with caution, but also with newfound clarity. It is in this clarity that we find our true allies, those who stand by us not for spectacle or gain, but for shared humanity and unconditional love. Through this ordeal, we're not hardened but more honed in to our intuition. We are wiser in our interactions and ever more grateful for the authenticity of a few, rather than the fickle attention of the many. Our journey continues, and with it, our story grows richer, instilled with the wisdom of hard-earned lessons and the grace of genuine kinship.

Good Advice – Take Back Control of Your Life

When grief strikes, you may find yourself standing at the crossroads of who you were and who you're becoming. The truth is, after a profound loss, you're never quite the same. A part of you might linger in the shadows of what used to be, yearning for the light-hearted ease you once knew. As you embrace this new chapter, you discover that the quiet spaces you now inhabit are not voids but sanctuaries for growth. Perhaps it is just part of my ongoing healing journey, but as I look at photos of us from before Violet passed, I feel as though that guy in the picture has lost his happy-go-lucky innocence. I am still an extra, extrovert but I need longer to myself afterwards. We also appreciate downtime more than we ever did before. We have found ourselves gravitating to smaller, more intimate interactions, rather than large events.

I have found that we have gained some new strengths along this journey. We have a newfound resilience that we did not possess in the past. Danielle and I are both very caring, compassionate people, but we would previously find ourselves overcommitting ourselves to others from an emotional standpoint. We have both always been a little on the sensitive side too, don't tell anyone. After almost losing Violet and Danielle, not much phases me. My threshold for what is meaningful and what is background noise is very defined now. My resilience is now not just a part of my story; in many ways, it has now become a defining trait, and bedrock of my being. I wear it quietly, not as armor, but as the very fabric of my character.

I feel like I can conquer anything in life as long as I have Danielle by my side. In some ways, I feel as though we have another shot at life together. Danielle and I have a new depth to our relationship. Even though we have only been together for about five years, we have decades' worth of battles together already. I feel a strength whispering in my ear that I can weather any storm, so long as the hands I hold are those that matter most. This resilience is our beacon, casting a light that helps to guide us through the darkness, promising that together, the voyage is not only endurable but surmountable.

My advice to anyone, especially those battling through something in life, is to focus on what matters most to you and your family. Do not let others define what that looks like for you. Take back control of your life from distractions, bad habits, fake friends, and toxic people. Feel free to recalibrate your priorities. Anchor yourself to what is essential, hold dear to the core of your life, and focus on your happiness. There is strength in choosing intimate conversations over spectacles, in savoring the soft murmur of conversation over the hassle of crowds. This isn't a retreat, but rather a strategic advance toward what truly enriches your soul. We have noticed that even as we have taken a step back, the people that want to be in our lives have stayed in sync with us. In this, there is freedom, a glorious escape from the chains of expectation and the liberation to truly live, and love, on your own terms.

CHAPTER 5

The Reset

Almost five months had passed since Violet's passing. I was starting to get my head above water at work, and Danielle was exploring the idea of returning to her profession soon. We were feeling a bit more optimistic after the reset of our life. We were reintroducing ourselves into our work, social engagements, and trying to put on a good face. This was our "face it until you make it" period, a mantra that echoed through our days as we tried to navigate the tumultuous sea of grief. As we stepped back into the ebb and flow of everyday life, each interaction felt like walking a tightrope, balancing between the world's expectations and the weight of our own hearts. Work beckoned with its familiar rhythms, social circles with their comforting banter, but underneath the surface lurked a tangle of emotions, ready to trip us at any mention of family.

In this chapter of our lives, we learned to face it until we made it. Smiles became our armor, and laughter our deflective shield. Yet, nothing tested our resolve quite like the innocent question that punctures the soul of any grieving parent: "Do you have children?" After the loss, we oscillated between great sadness, anger, and just holding it all together with a smile as our mask. One of the greatest challenges as we reacclimated was when people would ask us if we had children or inquire about our kids. It always felt so tense in the room around us, even for the good-natured people, and those who were simply looking out for us. People always felt awful after they asked us about our family, and we didn't want that either.

Danielle and I were trying to adapt to our new norms and making the best of each day. It felt like living a dual life, one of enduring deep private sorrow and one where we presented a composed façade to the outside world. We were starting to lean into our sense of adventure again, utilizing one of our favorite coping tools. We began to explore our city, other major California cities, and national parks in the Golden State. We felt great as we visited Yosemite and Sequoia National Park with some fantastic friends from Florida. Another reason we had a little more pep in our step was that we had decided to have faith and try to get pregnant again. I made all kinds of big-topic life suggestions to Danielle after Violet passed. I threw out topics ranging from adoption, to fostering, to trying again. Lucky for me, I am married to a very level-headed, logical little saint.

We ultimately decided to trust in God, in each other, and to allow ourselves to trust the process again. During this time, we were making intentional efforts to get out of the house a bit more, for the sake of our sanity. We just let life happen and let go. We found ourselves looking at a positive pregnancy test a few weeks later. We were happy about the positive result but were still numb, unable to fully embrace the joy after the loss of Violet a few months prior. After sharing the good news as "a gift" for my mother on Mother's Day, we only told a handful of other friends. For the next few weeks, we struggled mightily with the idea of a new child, as we were still deep in the claws of grief.

Just as quickly as we started to believe again, Danielle experienced a miscarriage. We were out at a busy Asian restaurant, dozens of people around. She returned from the restroom with a look of defeat on her face. I knew the second I saw her expression. At that moment, I felt like Danielle and I were alone in the restaurant, isolated on an island with our sadness. I gave her a big hug, and we both held back tears. We paid the check as quickly as we could and left. I remember the drive home feeling like it would not end. I was so sad, but I felt a compounded heartache because I knew what it took for Danielle to believe again. Life became a blurred rough patch for us for a while after that. As I reflect on this moment, it was a turning point for me. I felt that I had hit a new emotional low. It felt like we had some hope back in our life and were starting to taste the sweetness of happiness. I won't speak for my better half, but this is when depression really began to kick my butt.

I threw myself a pity party occasionally; anger and grief can make you ugly at times. I was not immune. "The guy that coached, mentored, and 'big-brothered' his whole life and never cared about having a child, but finally went for it. He failed. I failed. It just wasn't meant to be." All those terrible thoughts, the ones you would not let your friends have, they ran wild in my mind. I knew better, and I was certainly advised differently. I wondered if we could or even should try to conceive again. Unfortunately, it took me almost a year to shake these thoughts and feelings, to lift this mental fog. This is what I tell myself, but make no mistake, we have plenty of days where we still reflect with anger and extreme sadness.

For the well-intentioned, the news of our loss was a shockwave, rippling with discomfort and pity. Their faces mirrored the heartache we carried, a reminder that while our sorrow was ours alone to bear, its echoes reached far beyond us. 'The Reset' is not just a book chapter; it's a testament to our resilience in the face of such questions and the complex choreography of social graces we performed daily. It's about holding onto each other as the rest of the world unwittingly nudged at our wounds, reminding us that while Violet's physical presence was no longer with us, the impact of her existence was indelible, leaving a mark on every encounter, every whispered response, and every strained smile.

Coping Tools – Exercise: My Lifelong Sanctuary

Exercise has been more than just a physical activity for me; it's been a sanctuary, a place where I can find solace, strength, and clarity. From my earliest days growing up in a rough inner-city neighborhood, working out was a way to protect myself, to build a shield of lean mass that not only fortified my body but also bolstered my confidence. I was just a skinny kid, standing 6'2" but weighing only 140 lbs. By the time I reached the end of high school, I had managed to put on 50 lbs of lean muscle, transforming my frame and, more importantly, my self-image.

The satisfaction that came with working out was immediate, and it planted a seed that would grow into a lifelong passion. In my late teens and early 20s, I pushed my physical boundaries further, eventually reaching 230 lbs of lean mass at my biggest. But exercise wasn't just about aesthetics or physical strength; it was about control, discipline, and finding a place of refuge in the chaos of life. The gym became a sanctuary where I could channel my energy, clear my mind, and build the mental resilience that would later carry me through some of the toughest times in my life.

This passion for exercise naturally led me to pursue a career in personal training. I got my certification in Tampa, FL, and began working at Lifestyle Family Fitness, where I used my knowledge, skills, and experience to help others reach their physical peak. I saw firsthand how exercise could reshape not just bodies but lives. The transformation that occurs when someone starts to see themselves differently, to believe in their own strength and potential, is nothing short of miraculous. Helping others achieve that transformation became as fulfilling as any personal achievement I had reached in the gym.

But the impact of exercise on my life didn't stop there. It was the foundation that helped me step into the world of public service. My first job in local government was as the Fitness Coordinator for the City of Temple Terrace, FL. It was a chance opportunity, one that I might not have pursued if it weren't for my passion for fitness. This role allowed me to combine my love for exercise with a growing interest in serving the community. I quickly realized that recreation was about more than just physical activity; it was about building healthier, happier communities.

As my passion for public service grew, so did my commitment to education. I put myself through school in the evenings after work, completing my undergraduate degree in Business Administration over the course of 11 years. It was a long, challenging journey, but the discipline I had developed through years of strength training helped me push through. After that, the advanced degrees came more quickly, a Master's in Public Administration and a Doctor of Education (Ed.D) in Organizational Leadership.

Exercise was the cornerstone that supported all these achievements. It gave me the resilience to persevere through late-night study sessions, the energy to juggle work, school, and personal life, and the mental clarity to stay focused on my goals. It also provided a much-needed outlet during times of stress, a way to reset and recharge when life's demands felt overwhelming. Even now, in my early 40s, exercise remains my most powerful coping tool. Strength training several days a week keeps my body strong, but it's the mental and emotional benefits that I value most. Each morning begins with meditation and a ride on my Peloton, setting the tone for the day with a sense of accomplishment and calm. The sauna is another cherished part of my routine, a place where I can unwind, reflect, and let the heat melt away the stresses of the day.

This commitment to exercise has been more than just a personal pursuit; it has shaped my entire career. From those early days as a Fitness Coordinator, I've grown into various roles within local government—marketing, communications, economic development, and eventually city and county management. Each step along the way, I've relied on the discipline, resilience, and focus that exercise has instilled in me. Now, as I prepare to step into my newest role as the County Manager of Doña Ana County, New Mexico, I know that the same principles will guide me. This journey all started from my top coping tool, which will always be exercise. It's the thread that weaves through every chapter of my life, a constant source of strength and stability in a world that can often feel uncertain and overwhelming.

In the wake of unimaginable loss, when grief threatened to drown me, it was exercise that helped me keep my head above water. It was the one thing I could control when everything else felt out of my hands. Each rep, each pedal stroke, each drop of sweat was a step towards reclaiming my life, towards building a new sense of normalcy in the aftermath of tragedy. Exercise didn't just keep me physically strong; it kept me mentally resilient, giving me the strength to face each day and the hope that, no matter how deep the pain, I could endure.

For anyone else walking through the valley of grief, I can't recommend enough the power of physical activity. Whether it's lifting weights, running, cycling, or any other form of movement, exercise can be a lifeline. It's a way to process emotions, to find clarity in the midst of chaos, and to build the resilience needed to keep moving forward. For me it is not about the physical attributes, it's about the mind, the heart, and the spirit. Exercise is my sanctuary, and it can be yours too.

A Journal Journey – The Butterfly

My life's narrative now unfolds in two distinct chapters: B.V. (Before Violet) and A.V. (After Violet). The years before her birth were filled with their own hurdles, challenges that at the time felt significant but now seem trivial in comparison to the seismic shift brought on by Vio's passing. Before Violet, my days were a collection of personal victories and adversities, each one a small notch in the timeline of my life. None of these years had prepared me for the transformative odyssey of my first fatherhood experience. Her arrival was like the first flap of a butterfly's wings within the cocoon, subtle yet prophetic of a metamorphosis. In the time after Violet, each moment became a step in the delicate dance of grief and growth, a journey marked by the tension between holding on and letting go.

The butterfly, a creature of fleeting beauty, encapsulates the essence of Vio's journey. In its delicate form and transient life, the butterfly is both a symbol of fragility and profound transformation. Violet's life, brief as it was, is a poignant reminder that from the depths of despair can emerge a new strength, a new purpose. Like the butterfly that must endure the confinement of the cocoon before it can soar, I, too, find myself navigating the confines of loss, waiting for the day I can find some sense of peace again. Her presence is always with me, reminding me that even in the hardest moments, there's a reason to keep going.

The butterfly is more than just a symbol; it's a connection to the cycles of life and rebirth, to the fragile beauty of existence. It reminds me that even in the briefest of moments, there is significance and impact. Violet's life, like the flutter of a butterfly's wings, created ripples far beyond her short time with us. Each day that passes is a testament to her influence, to the love that continues to grow even in her absence. The memory of her is a soft, constant presence, a reminder that life, no matter how fleeting, leaves its mark. Every time I see a butterfly, I'm reminded of her brief yet profound impact on our lives. It's as if the universe is sending us little signs, letting us know that she's still with us, fluttering nearby, unseen but ever-present.

As I mentioned earlier in this book, the butterfly was also the symbol used at the hospital for the children who did not remain in our world. I noticed the butterfly logo outside our door at the hospital, a simple, almost unnoticed emblem that carried the weight of a universe of grief. I would later confirm with the staff that it was the emblem they used so others would know that we were parents who had lost our baby, as she morphed from caterpillar to butterfly. That small symbol, meant to convey so much in such a simple image, now carries with it the weight of our entire experience. It's a reminder of the fragility of life, of the delicate balance between hope and despair, and of the profound transformation that can arise from our darkest moments.

The violet-colored butterfly has since become a logo for Violet in a way. It's not just a symbol of her life but of the transformation that her life brought to ours. In the stillness that follows her passing, the image of the butterfly serves as a reminder of her brief yet impactful journey. I also use the purple butterfly logo that I originally sketched out as the symbol for The Violet Movement, the non-profit that we created in Violet's name and honor. This logo, this symbol of transformation and fragile beauty, is now the banner under which we march forward, carrying Violet's legacy into the world. It's a reminder that out of the cocoon of grief, something beautiful can emerge, that life, despite its losses, continues to flutter and fly, touching others in ways we may never fully understand.

The Violet Movement

The butterfly, delicate yet resilient, mirrors the journey of healing, fragile, easily bruised, yet capable of remarkable transformation. Violet's story is a testament to this resilience, to the power of love to transcend even the greatest losses. As I continue to navigate the A.V. chapter of my life, the butterfly remains a symbol of hope, a reminder that, like Violet, we all have the capacity to leave a lasting imprint on the world, no matter how brief our time here may be. Each day, as I carry her memory with me, I strive to live in a way that honors her legacy, embracing the transformation that her life and loss have inspired in me. The butterfly is not just a symbol of her but a symbol of the journey we all must take, a journey of growth, of change, and of finding beauty in the midst of pain.

Lessons Learned – Unhealthy Coping

One of the most difficult lessons I've learned through this journey is the complexity of coping mechanisms and the ways they can both help and hinder the healing process. After losing Violet and experiencing a miscarriage, I found myself reaching for whiskey as a means to dull the relentless pain that seemed to shadow every moment. It became a reluctant confidant, a coping tool that offered relief in moments when I felt too numb to cry and too angry to stay silent. Sitting in the dim light of our living room, a glass of whiskey in hand, I let the warmth of the alcohol dull the sharp edges of my grief. For a time, it seemed like the only thing that could take the edge off the day, offering a brief reprieve from the overwhelming emotions that threatened to consume me.

The evenings were the hardest. As the day would draw to a close and the world quieted down, the silence became unbearable. The stillness of the night seemed to amplify the void left by Violet's absence. Whiskey filled that void, at least temporarily. The first sip is like a warm embrace, softening the harsh reality that awaited me. It became a ritual of sorts, pouring a drink, sitting in the quiet, and letting the bourbon or rye wash over me, dulling the pain, if only for a little while. The thing about whiskey is that it never really heals anything. It just numbs you to the pain for a while, but the pain is always waiting on the other side of the glass. The more frequently I drank, the more I realized that the whiskey wasn't taking the pain away; it was just pushing it down, suppressing it, and in doing so, it was delaying my healing.

To be clear, I am a happily married, professional. I am not talking about getting passed out drunk or going out partying. Alcoholism runs in my family, and I went through that phase in my early 20's. Instead of 2 good pours of a high-end rye, on a Friday or Saturday, it looked more like 3 pours, 5 nights a week. When you are trying to balance being a good husband, community leader, employee, and maintain momentum in the gym; alcohol is the opposite of what I needed. I began to see that while the whiskey made the nights more bearable, it was robbing me of the chance to process my grief fully, to confront it head-on. I was stuck in a cycle of numbness, and each morning, as the fog of alcohol lifted, the pain was still there, sharper, more insistent, reminding me that I couldn't outrun my grief. Eventually, I had to face the reality that whiskey wasn't helping me move forward; it was holding me back, keeping me anchored to a place of sadness and regret.

I'm not proud of it, and I certainly don't advocate for alcohol as a coping tool. In fact, I would caution against it. However, in the spirit of being honest about the good, the bad, and the ugly, I need to acknowledge that for a period, whiskey was a part of my journey. It was the crutch I leaned on when the weight of our loss became too much to bear. I was fully aware that it wasn't the healthiest choice, but when you're in the trenches of grief, sometimes you grab onto whatever is within reach.

The support it offered was fleeting. Each morning, the harsh light of day would reveal the truth: the pain was still there, untouched and unresolved. I was merely postponing the inevitable, delaying the moment when I would have to confront my grief head-on. Thus, I began to realize that I needed to find healthier ways to cope with my grief. I needed ways that would help me heal instead of just numbing the pain temporarily. It took me a while to get there, and in the meantime, whiskey was a part of my journey. But eventually, I knew that I had to let it go if I was ever going to move forward.

This experience taught me the important lesson that coping mechanisms are not inherently good or bad; they are tools, and it's how we use them that determines their impact on our lives. Whiskey, for me, was a double-edged sword. It offered short-term relief, but at the cost of long-term healing. I had to learn to navigate this delicate balance, to recognize when a coping tool was serving me and when it was holding me back. It's a lesson that's applicable to many areas of life, not just in dealing with grief. Whether it's alcohol, work, or any other distraction we use to avoid confronting our pain, it's crucial to remain mindful of how these tools affect us.

Ultimately, the most important lesson I learned is that it's okay to not be okay. That's a tough pill to swallow for someone like me, who's always prided himself on being strong, on being the one who others can lean on. But after losing Violet and then the miscarriage, I had to come to terms with the fact that sometimes, strength isn't about holding it all together. Sometimes, strength is about letting yourself fall apart. For a long time, I tried to fight it. I tried to push through the pain, to pretend like I was okay, even when I wasn't. But all that did was make things worse. The more I tried to suppress my grief, the more it consumed me.

It wasn't until I started to allow myself to feel the pain that I began to heal. I learned that it's okay to have bad days, to have days where you just can't function. It's okay to cry, to scream, to feel like the world is crumbling around you. It's okay to acknowledge that you're not okay, that you're hurting, and that you need time to heal. Grief isn't something you can just get over. It's something you have to move through, and that process is messy and painful. It's also a necessary step. You can't outrun grief; it will always catch up to you eventually. By facing it head-on, by allowing yourself to feel the pain, you can begin to heal. That's one of the most important lessons I've learned: it's okay to not be okay, as long as you keep moving forward, even if it's just a little bit at a time.

In the end, I had to learn to forgive myself for reaching for extra glasses of whiskey in those dark moments. I had to give myself grace, recognizing that I was doing the best I could under the circumstances. But I also had to find the strength to put the glass down, to let go of that crutch, and to walk the path of healing on my own two feet. It wasn't easy, and it's still a journey I'm on, but I've learned that true healing comes from within. It comes from facing the pain, embracing the grief, and allowing yourself the time and space to heal. That's a lesson that will stay with me for the rest of my life.

Good Advice - Get Lost to Find Yourself

Travel has always been a cornerstone of our lives, a way to connect with the world and with each other. It's a love affair that has taken us to the far reaches of the globe, where we've immersed ourselves in different cultures, cuisines, and the wisdom of people from all walks of life. Through travel, we have learned the most profound lessons, ones that cannot be taught within the confines of our familiar surroundings. This section is a testament to the power of exploration in the healing process. Throughout my life, I've had the privilege of visiting 90 countries. Each journey has been an adventure, a chance to learn and grow, to see the world through a new lens. Nothing brings our family more joy than the sense of adventure that comes with discovering new places. During our pregnancy with Violet, we continued to embrace this passion, visiting six countries with our little girl within the safety of Danielle's womb. Those photos and memories are treasures that we hold close to our hearts.

In the aftermath of Violet's death on January 7th, 2023, travel became a lifeline for us. The grief was overwhelming, and we needed a way to reconnect with ourselves and each other. From that heart-wrenching day to the summer of 2024, we visited seven countries, each trip a step towards healing. One of the most memorable journeys was our trip to Istanbul in April 2023, during the holy time of Ramadan. Exploring Istanbul was a profound experience. The city, with its rich history and vibrant culture, provided a backdrop for us to rediscover the joy of life. We wandered through the bustling streets, the calls to prayer echoing in the air, a constant reminder of the city's spiritual heartbeat. We started our days feasting on local favorites on the European side of Istanbul, savoring the flavors that told stories of generations. The mornings were filled with the aroma of freshly baked simit and the rich, earthy taste of Turkish coffee.

As the day unfolded, we found ourselves crossing the Bosporus Sea to the Asian side of Istanbul. There, we indulged in an amazing Dim Sum lunch, a testament to the city's diverse culinary landscape. The experience of dining in two continents within a single day was surreal, a reminder of Istanbul's unique position at the crossroads of the world. The afternoon sun bathed the city in a golden glow as we made our way back to the European side, where the majestic Hagia Sophia awaited us. Our evenings were spent near this iconic landmark, sipping drinks and sharing delightful dinners that were a feast of flavors for these fervent foodies. The Hagia Sophia, with its towering minarets and grand domes, stood as a silent witness to our moments of joy and sorrow. For those two weeks, we were transported to another world, experiencing the magic of Ramadan in one of the world's most historic cities. It was exactly what we needed, a chance to get lost in the wonders of a new place, to find comfort in the beauty of exploration.

There is something truly unique about travel. It engages a different part of you, awakening a sense of wonder and curiosity that can often lie dormant in adulthood. This child-like fascination, the thrill of discovering something new, is a powerful antidote to the weight of grief. As we navigated the labyrinthine streets of Istanbul, we felt a connection to the world that reminded us we were part of something larger. It was a reminder that life, in all its complexity and beauty, continues.

Traveling during this period of profound loss allowed us to see the world anew. It was a way to honor Violet's memory, to carry her with us in every new experience. Each trip was a step towards healing, a chance to rebuild ourselves in the aftermath of tragedy. The exploration of new places and cultures provided a sanctuary where we could process our grief, away from the familiar reminders of our pain. As we moved through the bustling markets and serene mosques of Istanbul, we felt a sense of peace that had been elusive. The city's rhythm, its blend of the old and the new, mirrored our own journey of reconciling past and present. In the quiet moments of reflection, sitting by the Bosporus, we found the strength to keep moving forward.

Travel has long been associated with relaxation and enjoyment, but recent research has shown that it can also have a profound impact on mental health. A growing body of evidence suggests that travel can improve mood, reduce stress, and increase feelings of well-being. For instance, a study conducted by the University of East Anglia found that taking a vacation can reduce the risk of depression by up to 30%.

Those who vacationed at least twice a year were significantly less likely to experience symptoms of depression (University of East Anglia).

Similarly, research published in the journal *Personality and Individual Differences* indicated that regular travelers report higher levels of self-esteem and life satisfaction. The study surveyed over 1,500 individuals and discovered that those who traveled in the past year experienced greater well-being than those who had not (Milman, 2021). These findings are echoed by the World Health Organization, which states, "Travel contributes to a person's physical and mental health by providing opportunities for pleasure, relaxation, and interest" (World Health Organization, 2023). The sense of adventure and excitement that travel provides can be especially beneficial in our fast-paced world, offering a much-needed break from constant stress and distractions. Moreover, a 2018 study by researchers in Austria found that stress decreased and overall well-being improved for a period of 15 to 45 days after a vacation (Gump & Matthews, 2018).

One of the key ways travel improves mental health is by encouraging us to step out of our comfort zones and try new things. This can be invigorating, providing a sense of accomplishment and personal growth. By visiting new places and experiencing new cultures, we can learn more about ourselves and the world around us, fostering greater self-awareness and fulfillment. The evidence is clear, yet many people still adhere to the hustle mindset, where it is frowned upon to slow down and enjoy what the world has to offer. For some people, escaping their everyday to do nothing at a resort by a beautiful pool is the recharge they are looking for. For us, it is all about the mental stimulation of awakening the inner explorer in ourselves, and being entrenched as an ethnographer. Our goal is to gain a deep, holistic understanding of how people live, interact, and make sense of their world. We immerse ourselves in these diverse environments to learn about and appreciate the nuances of various cultures. Although you we are not formally conducting research, our approach to experiencing and understanding other cultures reflects the essence of what ethnographers do. This entrenchment contributes to a happier and more fulfilled life, and it does more for our minds than simply giving us a break. "When you travel, you are more curious and more open to new experiences. You learn to relate to people better because you have a need to interact with new people. And therefore, you have an influx of new ways of looking at things" (Brein, 2021).

For anyone grappling with loss or searching for meaning, I encourage you to get lost to find yourself. Travel opens your eyes to the world's vastness and diversity, reminding you that there is always more to see, more to learn, and more to experience. It's a way to honor those we've lost by living fully and embracing the adventure of life. As we continue our journey, each trip is a tribute to Violet. Her spirit accompanies us, guiding us to new places and new experiences. Through The Violet Movement and our travels, we ensure that her legacy lives on, inspiring us and others to explore the world with open hearts and curious minds. In getting lost, we have found a way to heal, to celebrate life, and to keep Violet's memory alive in the most vibrant and meaningful way possible.

CHAPTER 6
The Weight of Absence

As the weeks turned into months after Violet's passing, the weight of her absence settled into every corner of our lives. It was a weight that pressed down on us, a constant reminder of what was lost and of the dreams that would never come to fruition. I've navigated the shadows of depression at various stages of my life, during childhood, as a teenager, and as a young adult. Yet, none of these episodes prepared me for the monumental wave of sorrow that struck me as a first-time father over forty. The joy of anticipating Violet's arrival was swiftly overshadowed by the heart-shattering grief that followed her loss, compounded further by the miscarriage that came after.

Depression is a formidable force. It has this insidious ability to strip even the most confident among us of our self-assurance, reducing poise to rubble in moments. Previously, I discussed the reset that comes after grief, a necessary element of any rebuild. But what happens when the very foundation of your life feels like it's been torn apart? When every day feels like wading through quicksand, and the routine tasks that once seemed so simple now demand monumental effort? This is the stage of grief where nothing comes easy, where the familiar autopilot of daily life is nowhere to be found.

My usual spark of high energy and natural positivity now required a deliberate ignition, a conscious effort to fan the flames of optimism. Each day was a battle to find even a sliver of joy, to reclaim some semblance of the person I once was. The weight of absence is not just the absence of Violet, it's the absence of the life we had imagined, the future that was so abruptly and cruelly taken from us.

A phenomenon that I found particularly striking over the last two years was how uncomfortable people became when I brought up depression, even if I was the one introducing the topic. This discomfort seemed strange considering that nearly one-third of Americans will have been diagnosed with depression at some point in their lives. Why is it that we can talk so openly about physical injuries, yet when it comes to mental health, there's still this stigma, this unspoken rule that we should keep our struggles to ourselves? When someone limps into a room on crutches or has their arm in a sling, there's often open dialogue about the injury, sometimes even a bit of humor. Why is it so different when it comes to mental health challenges?

We are blessed beyond measure to have the support circle that we do. In the early days of our grief, our friends and family rallied around us, bringing meals, sending messages, and simply being there. But as time passed, the steady stream of support began to wane. It's not out of a lack of kindness or empathy, but a general misconception that grief has an expiration date. By the fourth month, the check-ins had dwindled, and the palpable empathy once offered by friends and colleagues seemed to evaporate, leaving expectations of normalcy in its wake. Yet here we were, still grappling with the profound transformation that loss had brought to our home.

Though we yearned to return to some semblance of our former selves, the truth was that the foundation of our being had been altered forever. The feelings of isolation deepened as it became increasingly clear that while the world was moving on, we were still stuck, trying to navigate the quagmire of our grief. The reality was that I was not my best self at work for most of 2023. Life hit the reset button on us, but we did not reboot properly. It seemed like everyone else was operating at a different speed, while we were still struggling with an older, outdated operating system.

We could feel it when our grace period was expiring, with friends, with the community, and in the office. I heard rumblings that some people were starting to become frustrated that we weren't closer to our former selves by now. How could we be? The loss of a child is not something you simply move on from. It's not a chapter you close and then continue with the story. It's a permanent mark on your soul, a scar that will never fully heal.

In the trenches of depression, simplicity became our mantra and joy our quest. Happiness, I've come to realize, is not just a brief state of mind but a daily commitment, especially in the company of those who nourish our souls. This chapter is a call to action for all who navigate the murky waters of depression. Anchor yourself with simplicity and surround yourself with soul-enriching people. Rebuilding oneself after a devastating loss is not about recapturing who you were in the past.

It's about forging a new path, one that acknowledges and incorporates the lessons and changes brought about by grief, loss, and depression.

The person who emerges from this process is invariably changed, tempered by experience, and stronger through an improved level of resilience. I've learned that the journey doesn't have a neat conclusion or a definitive endpoint. Grief is not a linear experience. It ebbs and flows like the ocean tide, each wave a reminder of what was lost, but also of what remains. Rebuilding after loss and through grief is about finding a new balance in life, one where joy and sadness can coexist.

This realization requires an acceptance that is difficult to cultivate, but it is critical for growth. We must strive to accept that while the severe pain of loss diminishes over time, the love and the missing endure forever. In the months following our profound loss, I found that not only the landscape of my external world had changed, but my internal world had shifted dramatically too. Things that once seemed of monumental importance now paled in comparison to the vivid starkness of grief. This shift in perspective was disorienting, yet it brought clarity about what truly matters in life, family, health, and happiness.

This insight led me to reflect on the nature of support and empathy. Support from others is not just about being there when tragedy strikes. True support is understanding that recovery is a complex, ongoing process. The things that help to cope one day may not be as effective the following month. It is about being present without the constant need for progress updates. It's about offering space when needed and closeness when sought. In professional settings, too, I now advocate more for a cultural shift towards greater empathy and openness. We spend a significant portion of our lives at work, yet the business world often feels ill-equipped to handle the emotional turbulence of its workforce. By fostering an environment where employees feel safe to express their vulnerabilities, we cultivate not only individual well-being but also a more supportive, engaged, and ultimately productive workplace. I am blessed to have an organization that shares these same values.

As we navigated this journey, Danielle and I often found ourselves retreating into our cocoon, seeking solace in the quiet moments at home. Like the butterfly, we often opted to keep our fragile wings from getting wet in the storm. We learned to rest and regroup to fly again another day. We would adapt to start venturing out more, to reengage with the world at our own pace. This was a big step for us as it required a shower, clean clothes, and at least a forced smile. We found joy in small gatherings, in the beauty of nature, and in the simple acts of kindness that we exchanged with others. Each step outside our comfort zone was a small victory, a reaffirmation of life's persistence.

Reflecting on all these aspects, it becomes clear that healing is not just about moving past grief but growing around it, allowing it to become part of your story without letting it define you. It's about learning to dance in the rain, even when the storm seems unending. Through it all, it's about holding onto the love that binds us, the love that outlasts even the deepest sorrow. It is my hope that we can change the narrative around mental health, depression, and grief. Let's build more communities where openness replaces avoidance, where support is unwavering, and where every individual feels valued. Let's continue to lead with love in every aspect of our lives, even when our hearts are heavy from the weight of absence.

Coping Tools – Indulging

Speaking of weight, for better and worse, food became a coping tool for me during our road to recovery. We've always been foodies, relishing the discovery of new dishes, whether in a hidden gem of a restaurant or a Michelin-starred establishment. But in the wake of our loss, our passion for cuisine became a coping mechanism. The communal act of sharing meals, especially during the initial phase of grief, brought a semblance of normalcy in a world turned upside down. However, that normalcy came with a cost, as the emotional relationship with food grew more complex.

I found myself eating not just for sustenance or pleasure but as a way to fill the void that grief had carved into my life. Food became a temporary salve, a momentary distraction from the overwhelming sadness that threatened to consume me. The meal train set up by our wonderful friends was a blessing, bringing us comfort when we could barely muster the energy to cook for ourselves. But with those meals came the creeping realization that I was using food to mask my pain. Desserts, rich comfort foods, and indulgent dinners became a nightly ritual, a way to feel something other than sorrow, even if just for a moment.

In the year following Violet's death, I gained about ten pounds. To some, this might seem insignificant, but for someone who has spent a lifetime dedicated to fitness and health, it was a jarring reminder of how far I had strayed from my usual discipline. As a former personal trainer and athlete, I know better than anyone that you can't outrun your fork. Despite my daily workouts and Peloton rides, the comfort foods were catching up with me. It was a stark realization that even when you're doing everything right in the gym, your diet plays an equally important role in your overall well-being.

The connection between food and emotion is a powerful one, and in times of stress or sadness, it's easy to fall into the trap of overeating. There's a reason we call them "comfort foods"—they offer a temporary sense of relief, a momentary pleasure that distracts from the pain. I've learned, that comfort is fleeting, and the long-term effects can be detrimental to both physical and mental health. It's a cycle that's hard to break, especially when the world around you feels so out of control. Food becomes one of the few things you can control, and in that sense, it can be both a refuge and a trap.

While whiskey, which we discussed earlier, played a role in lowering inhibitions, making it easier to indulge in overeating, it's important to recognize the deeper emotional currents that drive these behaviors. I share this not to focus on the physical implications but to highlight the emotional relationship we often have with food, especially during times of grief and stress. It's a reminder that our eating habits are often a reflection of our inner state and that finding balance is a crucial part of the healing process.

In the wake of loss, the immediate comfort of food often outweighed these considerations. It was a way for us to feel, even if momentarily, a sense of pleasure amidst the pervasive sadness. But as time went on, I realized that this coping mechanism was not sustainable. It was not just about the extra pounds; it was about the underlying grief that was driving these choices. I knew I had to confront the emotions I was trying to bury beneath layers of comfort food. I had to find healthier ways to cope, ways that would nourish not just my body but my soul as well.

The truth is, food and whiskey can be part of the healing process, but they must be approached with mindfulness. It's okay to find comfort in a good meal or a glass of whiskey, but it's also important to recognize when it's time to find other sources of solace. Balance is key, and that means finding ways to nourish your body and mind in a way that supports long-term healing.

A Journal Journey – The Cost of Ambition

Today is May 25, 2023, and I am struggling with a lot of emotions and what-ifs as I sit in the empty nursery and hold my daughter's ashes on my lap. If vasa previa is detectable, why is it still missed by medical professionals so often? Why did our tenured doctor miss this? Should we have seen another specialist for a second opinion? What if I hadn't taken the job in California? I know we would have had better medical care in Atlanta than we currently do in Bakersfield. Would the medical staff in Atlanta have caught the vasa previa that ultimately killed Violet and nearly took Danielle? I know it's not fair to myself to play the "what-if game." However, it's also impossibly difficult not to do so.

As a parent, you do everything in your power to provide a good life for your children. The goal is always to give them a childhood better than the one you experienced. This is something I struggle with, especially now in my pursuit of fatherhood. While it will be a pretty cool moment to hear my child eventually say, "My Daddy runs the county," I can't help but wonder if my ambitions have come at too great a cost. As a County Manager, I lead all day-to-day operations for the county. But by the time my child is old enough to have these conversations, I will likely not be in the same physical shape I am in today, despite my work ethic and best efforts. In general, most people are in their athletic prime in their 20s and 30s. Conversely, most are still finding their way and climbing the corporate ladder in those same years.

When you are incredibly ambitious, it is both a blessing and a curse. It is honestly an ongoing battle in my mind that has felt amplified through our loss, depression, and the awful "what-if" questions. Ambition is complex and complicated because it simultaneously is a driving force for an individual's success. The more ambitious you are, the higher you can raise your professional ceiling and earning potential. This puts you in a better position to fuel your passions and projects, but most importantly, to be better suited to provide for your family. However, it also brings an insatiable quest for more, and the constant pursuit of what is next. I've had some candid talks with people that I respect and love, as they have challenged me with the question, "What is enough?" When will I be satisfied with what we have? The truth is, I am completely satisfied in most ways, as Danielle and I have respectfully exceeded most expectations of what our parents probably had for us. But now, this conundrum is exacerbated because of our attempts to get pregnant again. Now, it feels like I have so many more mountains to climb and miles to go before I will be in a position where I can feel satisfied about the type of life I want our family to have.

Lessons Learned – Sit with the Pain

In the tangled web of grief, there's a particular stretch that winds through the darkness of pain. Here, in the depths, there is no shortcut, no fast track to the light at the end. This is the path of sitting with the pain, where the air is thick with the weight of loss, and every breath is a reminder of what was and what will never be again. You can't circumvent the grief process, much as you might wish to. It's a journey that demands every ounce of your presence. Feel the frustration. Numbing the pain isn't a realistic long-term or healthy option. Recognize and realize that things are not fair. It's a reality, life isn't fair. I say that from a realistic place, not one of sympathy or a grief-burdened place. This is also where faith becomes part of my headspace. I lament with God. Part of my lament is the process of deeply remembering Violet.

I've learned the importance of sitting with the pain. It's a process not of escaping, but of facing the harsh, unforgiving reality head-on. The focus is not on fleeing from the agony but embracing it. The pain you feel is the love you give, a testament to the depth of the bond that was formed. It's a hard truth, an echo of the grand paradox of life, that joy and pain are intertwined. The love that brought such warmth now brings an unfathomable chill of absence. Yet, this is the love that demands to be felt, to be honored in its fullness, even when it tears at the framework of your heart. Life isn't fair, a truth that's both simple and immensely complex. This unfairness isn't just a grief-stricken realization; it's a fundamental truth of human existence.

Sitting with the pain means acknowledging it, giving it space to breathe within you. It's the courageous act of staying present with your sorrow, of allowing yourself the dignity of your tears. This is the place where faith might whisper to you, not in grand proclamations or revelations, but in the silent communion of shared grief. It's a space where the sacred can coexist with the suffering, where lament is a form of prayer, and remembrance is a rite for the lost. This journey through pain is where my faith intersects with my grief. In my moments of deepest sorrow, I turn to God, not for answers, but for space to mourn. It's in these conversations with the divine that I find a place to voice my anger, my confusion, and my profound sadness. It's in these sacred moments of raw honesty that I allow myself to dive deep into the happiness of our pregnancy, to feel her presence and acknowledge her absence. This is not a process of moving on but moving through. It is a journey where each step is heavy with loss yet lightened by the bittersweet joy of remembrance.

To those walking this path now, allow yourself to feel the pain. This process is not easy, nor is it linear, but it is a necessary part of the journey toward healing. Feel the frustration, the burning injustice of a universe that seems indifferent to individual heartbreak. Yet, within this confrontation with life's inherent unfairness, there is a powerful act of defiance. To lament is not to accept but to protest, to rage against the dying of the light with every fiber of your being. This is an invitation to those enduring the sharp sting of loss: do not rush through the stages, do not avoid the pain. Instead, find the strength to sit with it, to let it shape you in ways you never imagined possible. Here, in this sacred space of suffering, you will learn lessons that are hard-won but invaluable. This isn't the denial of pain, but an acknowledgment of its transformative power. And in the solemn stillness of your heartache, you will find the courage to continue, to heal not by leaving the pain behind, but by integrating it into the narrative of your life, a novel where your loved one's spirit forever endures.

Good Advice – Fight for Your Happiness, Every Single Day

Navigating life's tumultuous seas, each wave brings its own trials, from the gentle ripples of everyday frustrations to the towering swells of profound grief. It's a journey where the quest for happiness is as vital as it is complex. This section is an earnest manifesto to claim joy as a fundamental right, not as a passing luxury. Imagine life as an arcade game, where happiness is the ultimate high score. If that is the case, why do so many of us pump our coins into machines that pay out in stress or tokens of fleeting pleasures? We chase after high-paying jobs, status symbols, and the next big thing, forgetting that these are the bonus points, not the main objective. The real win is in the laughter that fills your home, the peace that settles in your heart, and the love that wraps around you like a warm blanket on a cold night.

It's important to remember that happiness is a bold endeavor in a world that often values material wealth over emotional well-being. It's about choosing the people who celebrate your quirks, who champion your dreams, and who hand you a metaphorical sword to fend off the dragons of doubt. Prioritize those who not only applaud your achievements but also sit with you in the trenches when life's script takes a tragic turn. Take it from someone who has basked in the sunshine of mild success and been drenched by the downpour of hardship: happiness is not a static state. It's an active pursuit, a series of choices that align with the heart's compass. Like a cunning strategist in the game of life, deploy your resources toward pursuits that kindle your spirit. Simplify, not as a sacrifice, but as a strategy to make room for true joy.

In this fight for happiness, wield your weapons of gratitude, laughter, and love. Embrace the absurdity of chasing a balloon on a windy day, the peace that comes from your favorite author, or simply the satisfaction of a perfectly brewed cup of coffee. Take detours down paths lined with the things that make your soul sing, whether it's a passion project or an afternoon nap in a sunbeam. Recognize the currency of smiles, the wealth of a quiet moment, and the luxury of being authentically you. Curate your life with the same care you would a vibrant garden, knowing that while not every plant will thrive, the effort to cultivate beauty is never wasted. Surround yourself with the people, ideas, and things that make your heart feel like it's bursting with contentment, you are the creator of your own happiness.

In the grand scheme, whether you're a titan of industry or a champion of the home front, your happiness is the trophy that really matters. It's the laughter that echoes long after the room has emptied, that sigh of satisfaction at the end of a day well-lived, and the resilience that springs from knowing that even amidst the battles, you've chosen to dance in the rain. So go on, fight for your happiness with the tenacity of a superhero in a cape, because in this life, you're the hero of your own epic tale. We feel that the story of Violet, and our family's journey, can become a powerful testament to the resilience of the human spirit, the enduring nature of love, and the profound impact one life, no matter how brief, can have on the world. Through our narrative, we hope you will learn that even amidst the most tumultuous times, there are moments of clarity, peaks of joy, and the continuous thread of love that holds it all together.

CHAPTER 7

Helping Hands

In the tapestry of our story, there are threads of grief that are inextricably woven with the threads of love and support from others. It is unimaginable for us to share our journey without paying homage to the generous efforts, the outpouring of support, and the compassion we received from friends, neighbors, colleagues, and strangers alike. This chapter is a heartfelt tribute to those who lifted us when we could barely stand, those who helped us navigate the darkest days of our lives.

When we moved to Bakersfield, California, we were embarking on a new chapter, full of promise and hope. We had only lived in this new community for six months before Violet passed, and we were still in the process of finding our footing. Little did we know that this community, still new to us, would become our lifeline in the wake of unimaginable loss. Bakersfield, 2,200 miles away from our previous home, became more than just a new city, it became a sanctuary where we found a family of friends, colleagues, and neighbors who embraced us in our time of need.

In the aftermath of Violet's passing, our vulnerability became a bridge that connected us to the hearts of those around us. Despite the brevity of our time in Bakersfield, the warmth we received was akin to the comfort of lifelong friendships. The meal trains that appeared like clockwork, the soft chime of the doorbell signaling another thoughtful gift, and the silent strength of a supportive presence in a room still echoing with our heartache, all of these gestures sewed us into the fabric of the community. As a local government leader, I've always valued the story of communities showing up and leaning in for others. But to be on the receiving end of such love and support was an entirely new, humbling experience.

Our journey of grief was profoundly shaped by the kindness of others. We've experienced countless stories of compassion that made us feel like we belonged in this place, even when we were still strangers to many. It's an odd feeling for us, as people who have always been givers, to find ourselves as the recipients of so much love. Yet, this chapter of our lives taught us that home isn't just a place; it's the people who anchor you when the storms of life hit the hardest. The narrative of our time in Bakersfield weaves the personal into the professional, underscoring the human side of city management and the deep connections that can form in a short time, influencing both our lives and my leadership philosophy.

As the days turned into weeks and the weeks into months, we found that the steady stream of support began to wane, as is natural with the passage of time. However, certain groups and communities remained steadfast in their support, becoming pillars of strength for us as we navigated our new normal. Danielle found immense comfort and peace in MOPS (Moms of Preschoolers), a group she had joined when she was pregnant with Violet. Even after our loss, Danielle continued to be a part of this group, and it became an incredibly helpful space for her to heal. The women of MOPS, with their shared experiences of motherhood, both its joys and its heartbreaks, provided a sanctuary where Danielle could express her grief and find solace among those who understood.

In addition to MOPS, we found support in various grief groups, loss groups, book clubs, and through the broader Bakersfield community. These groups became our lifeline, helping us to find our way back to as close to normal as we would ever be again. They reminded us that while our journey was uniquely painful, we were not alone. We were surrounded by people who cared, who showed up even when it was uncomfortable or difficult, and who walked beside us as we worked to rebuild our lives.

Our communities have been an unexpected yet remarkable support system that emerged during our most trying times. Despite our heartbreak, we must acknowledge the monumental moments of human kindness we have experienced. These experiences have reinforced our faith in humanity and our belief that there are far more good people in the world than those who are malevolent in nature. We've felt the goodness of strangers near and far, and we are in awe of the compassion, kindness, and sincere sympathy that so many have shown us.

As we continued our journey of adjustment, we leaned on each other more as the empathy of others naturally began to wane after a few months. We adapted to our new life, accepting that it would be without Violet. Our frustrations, sadness, and anger came and went in waves, and we realized that grief is not a problem to be solved but a presence to be acknowledged. We learned that while the initial surge of community support might fade, the deep connections we had formed would remain, anchoring us as we moved forward.

LIFE IS ABOUT CHANGING AND GROWING

YOU'VE CHANGED

WE'RE SUPPOSE TO

This chapter is about the gradual, grudging shift from the rawness of immediate loss to the enduring ache of absence, navigating a world less attuned to our pain as time moved on. There is an omnipresent pressure—a duality of grief's persistence and life's insistence on moving forward. But through it all, we have found that the human spirit is adaptable, and with the help of others, we have begun to find new routines and meanings in life post-loss.

As we reflect on this journey, we are filled with immense gratitude. Gratitude for the people who helped us find our way, for the community that embraced us, and for the strength we found in each other. We are a testament to the power of helping hands and the profound impact that compassion and kindness can have on those who are struggling to find their way back to the light.

Coping Tools: The Violet Movement

In the wake of Violet Françoise Andrews' brief yet profoundly impactful life, my wife Danielle and I found ourselves grappling with an unimaginable void. The grief was a weight we carried daily, a silent, dark companion in every room, every conversation, every quiet moment. As we navigated this new reality, we sought a way to channel our sorrow into something meaningful. We wanted a way to honor Violet's memory and ensure that her brief time with us would have a lasting impact. This search led us to one of the most significant coping mechanisms in our journey through grief: the creation of The Violet Movement.

The Violet Movement was born out of our need to keep Violet's spirit alive, to transform our grief into a force for good. It became more than just a way to cope; it became a mission, a purpose that anchored us in the storm of our loss. Establishing this nonprofit wasn't merely about finding solace in action; it was about making a deliberate choice to inject love, kindness, and opportunity into the world in Violet's name. The foundation's core mission is to offer scholarships to students in need, reflecting our family's passions and history. In doing so, we ensure that Violet's legacy is not only remembered but also serves as a catalyst for future growth and community enrichment.

The process of setting up The Violet Movement was both cathartic and challenging. Every decision, whether it was designing the logo, defining the scholarship criteria, or outlining the mission, felt like a conversation with Violet. It was our way of involving her in our daily lives, of keeping her present in the choices we made. The foundation became a way to continue Violet's story, not as a tale of loss, but as a legacy of impact.

Why scholarships, you might ask? Education has always held a special place in our hearts. It has the power to transform lives, to open doors that would otherwise remain closed. By providing scholarships, we are planting seeds of change that will grow and branch out into the community, much like the branches of a sturdy, enduring tree. Each scholarship granted is a testament to Violet's lasting influence, an influence that extends far beyond the confines of our personal lives and into the broader world where we can cast a wider net to do more good.

The Violet Movement is more than just a coping tool; it is a living, breathing legacy. It allows us to talk about Violet openly, to celebrate her life, and to share her story with those who benefit from the foundation's work. It keeps her memory alive in the most active and positive way possible. Moreover, it provides us with comfort, knowing that her name will be spoken in gratitude and that her influence will be felt long into the future. This foundation is our way of ensuring that

Violet's spirit continues to touch lives, inspiring hope and providing opportunities for others.

Through The Violet Movement, we have established a range of scholarships, each reflecting core values and experiences that are deeply personal to us. These scholarships are more than just financial support; they are embodiments of the qualities that define human resilience and compassion, courage in the face of adversity, dedication to helping others, and the quiet strength of those who make a difference without seeking recognition.

Each scholarship ties back to a piece of our journey and our desire to honor Violet's memory in a way that extends beyond our own lives. Whether it's supporting individuals who have overcome significant challenges, celebrating those who lead with love and kindness, or raising awareness about the condition that claimed our daughter's life, these scholarships serve as living legacies. They are tributes to the qualities we hold dear and the lessons we have learned through our own trials. By empowering others to pursue their dreams and make a positive impact on their communities, we ensure that Violet's spirit continues to inspire and uplift.

Each of these scholarships serves as a beacon of hope, a way to empower and uplift individuals from diverse backgrounds. They encourage recipients to pursue their aspirations with determination and a sense of community support. Through these scholarships, Violet's legacy lives on, touching lives and making a difference in the world.

As this chapter unfolds, it becomes clear that transforming grief into action is about more than just healing; it's about making a difference. It's about shifting the narrative from what could have been to what will be because of Violet. The Violet Movement doesn't just bear her name; it carries forward her essence, her potential, every day through the lives of those it touches. To other grieving families looking for a way to honor their loved ones, consider this: turning your loss into a lifeline for others not only helps you heal but also creates an enduring tribute that can change lives. Your loved one's name, and more importantly, their spirit, can continue to play a vital role in the world, inspiring hope and providing opportunities for others. In this way, love transcends the physical and becomes a lasting legacy.

As we approach the launch of another set of scholarships this year, our hearts are heavy with the weight of missing Violet, but also filled with pride for what The Violet Movement has accomplished. This chapter isn't just our story, it's an invitation to all who have felt the sting of loss to find a path forward that honors memory with action, ensuring that no life, however brief, is without a meaningful legacy.

Journal Journey – July 15, 2023

It's been half a year since we lost Violet, and nearly two months since the miscarriage. I'm sitting here with a glass of whiskey, the ice melting slowly as I swirl the amber liquid around the glass. The quiet in the room is deafening, almost as if the world itself has come to a standstill, leaving me alone with my thoughts and the relentless ache in my chest. The days seem to bleed into one another, each indistinguishable from the last, a continuous loop of numbness and routine. I'm going through the motions, showing up at work, engaging in conversations, but it feels like I'm living in a shadow, a version of myself that's hollow and detached.

In the stillness of these moments, it's like I'm transported back to that hospital room, reliving the nightmare on an endless loop. The memory of that day is a constant presence, haunting me, anchoring me to a place I desperately want to escape but cannot. I watch Danielle, this incredible woman, trying to piece together a semblance of normalcy. Her resolve amazes me, and I want to be that pillar of strength for her, to be the husband she needs, but I'm stuck—frozen in time, weighed down by a grief that feels insurmountable.

The miscarriage was a devastating blow, a cruel reminder that joy can be as fleeting as it is precious. It's left me reeling, angry at everything and everyone. I'm angry at God for allowing this to happen, at myself for not being able to prevent it, at the universe for its cold indifference. It feels like I'm constantly teetering on the edge of breaking down, barely holding it together from one moment to the next. I know this can't go on. I'm aware that the path I'm on leads nowhere good, but I'm at a loss for how to change course. The pain is overwhelming, and the whiskey, for now, is my only refuge, numbing the sharp edges of my sorrow, even if just for a little while. But deep down, I know that this is a temporary fix, a crutch that's keeping me from confronting the real work of healing. I need to find a way out of this darkness, to reclaim some semblance of peace, not just for myself, but for Danielle, for us.

But tonight, the weight of it all is too much, and the thought of facing tomorrow feels impossible. So I take another sip, letting the warmth of the whiskey distract me from the cold reality I'm living in, and I pray that somehow, someway, tomorrow will be just a little bit easier.

Lessons Learned – It's Okay to Not Be Okay

One of the most humbling lessons I've had to learn through all of this is that it's okay to not be okay. For someone who's always prided himself on being strong, on being the rock that others can lean on, this realization was nothing short of earth-shattering. I've spent my entire life trying to be the steady hand in the storm, the one who could weather any hardship with grace and resilience. But after losing Violet, and then the miscarriage, I had to confront a truth that I'd been avoiding for far too long: sometimes, strength isn't about keeping it all together. Sometimes, real strength is about letting yourself fall apart.

For the longest time, I resisted this truth. I tried to soldier on, to bury my pain beneath a veneer of stoicism, convincing myself that if I just kept moving, kept pushing forward, the grief would eventually fade. But the more I tried to suppress it, the more it festered, growing stronger and more consuming. It wasn't until I allowed myself to truly feel the depth of my pain, to sit with it, to acknowledge its presence in my life, that I began to understand the importance of this process.

I learned that it's okay to have bad days, days where you can't function, where just getting out of bed feels like an impossible task. It's okay to cry until your body is exhausted, to scream at the injustice of it all, to feel like your world is crumbling around you. It's okay to question everything, to be angry, to be lost. Grief isn't something you can just get over or push through; it's something you have to move through, and that journey is messy, unpredictable, and deeply painful. But it's also an essential part of healing.

In this process, I've had to learn to give myself grace, to understand that healing isn't a straight line. There are good days and bad days, moments of clarity followed by moments of despair, and that's okay. What's important is that I keep moving, even if it's just one small step at a time. It's okay to not be okay, as long as I keep trying to find my way out of the darkness. I'm learning that it's not about getting back to who I was before all of this, it's about becoming someone new, someone who has been shaped by this loss but not defined by it.

Good Advice - Seasons Greetings

Reflecting on the past year, Danielle and I have found ourselves grappling with an intense internal struggle. The holiday season, particularly Thanksgiving and Christmas, cast a stark light on the depth of our grief over Violet's absence. What is typically a time of joy and togetherness was overshadowed by profound sorrow and a palpable sense of loss. We faced a complex mix of emotions; anger, sadness, and moments where we couldn't help but feel sorry for ourselves. While we know these feelings are common among those who have lost a child, that understanding did little to ease the heaviness we carried through the season.

Despite the weight of our grief, we managed to navigate Christmas by leaning deeply into the support of our loved ones. We allowed ourselves the space to mourn in our own ways, surrounding ourselves with people who offered genuine comfort and understanding. Choosing to spend time with those who truly uplifted us played a crucial role in our ability to cope, providing moments of peace and solace amidst the pain. It was a deliberate and necessary choice, one that reminded us of the healing power of community and compassion.

As New Year's Eve approached, we felt a subtle yet significant shift in our outlook. Celebrating with some of our closest friends, we found ourselves eager to leave the hardships of the past year behind and look forward with cautious optimism. There was a growing sense of anticipation for what the future might hold, including our hopes and efforts to expand our family once more. Balancing this newfound hope with the enduring grief of losing Violet was, and continues to be, a delicate endeavor. We often find ourselves navigating a complex emotional landscape, striving to honor Violet's memory while allowing space for new dreams and possibilities. It requires patience and grace, both with ourselves and each other, as we learn to embrace joy alongside our sorrow.

One of the most challenging aspects of our healing process has been recognizing that not everyone knows how to support us in our grief, including some family members and close friends. Grief is an uncomfortable and often uncharted territory, leaving many unsure of what to say or do. We understand this uncertainty all too well, having been on both sides of it ourselves. This realization has underscored the importance of prioritizing our mental health and well-being by intentionally surrounding ourselves with those who offer genuine support and allow us to be our authentic selves, even when we're not at our best.

This journey has taught us valuable lessons about the evolving nature of relationships. Some individuals we expected to lean on during our darkest moments were unable to provide the support we needed, which was difficult to accept. However, this opened our eyes to the incredible kindness and understanding extended by others, acquaintances, old friends we hadn't connected with in years, and even strangers, who stepped forward to become our pillars of strength. Their unexpected support has been a source of immense comfort, helping us navigate this challenging time with compassion and resilience.

We have come to highly value and encourage embracing support wherever it arises. Relationships naturally ebb and flow through different seasons of life, and it's okay when longtime friends fade into the background for a time. This doesn't diminish their importance or the roles they may play in the future; it's simply part of life's intricate tapestry. Embracing those who show up for us now has been both healing and empowering, reinforcing our belief that support and understanding can come from the most unexpected places.

Learning to focus on the present and appreciate the people who stand by us today has been a liberating experience. We've let go of expectations and disappointments tied to those who couldn't be there in the ways we hoped, choosing instead to surround ourselves with love and support that truly nourishes our souls. This shift in perspective has not only aided our healing but also strengthened our connections with those who have walked alongside us through our grief and hopes for the future.

CHAPTER 8

Cycles of Life

As the seasons of our lives shifted, Danielle and I found ourselves caught in the intricate dance of life's cycles, a dance where moments of profound loss intertwined with the promise of new beginnings. After Violet's passing and the miscarriage, grief settled over us like a thick fog, making it difficult to see beyond the pain. Yet, as time moved forward, so did we, stepping cautiously into a new season, one marked by a delicate balance of joy and sorrow.

2024 brought a much needed reprieve from the heaviness that had weighed us down. We embarked on a series of adventures with some of our closest friends, exploring the breathtaking beauty of California's wine country, Sequoia National Park, and Yosemite. These outings were more than just a distraction, they were a lifeline, a chance to reconnect with the world and with each other. The awe-inspiring landscapes provided a sense of peace that had eluded us for months, offering moments of lightness amidst the darkness we carried.

However, even in these moments of joy, a nagging intuition lingered in the back of my mind. I couldn't shake the feeling that something more was happening, that life was about to throw us another curveball. It wasn't long before my instincts were confirmed.

Danielle was pregnant again. Here we go, buckle up everyone. I like theme parks and all, being from central Florida. However, I knew that this ride was going to further test our emotional limits.

The news hit us with a rush of emotions, from cautious excitement to a deep, lingering fear. We had been here before, with Violet, and we knew all too well how fragile these early moments of hope could be. Yet, despite our anxiety, we allowed ourselves to embrace the joy of the moment, to feel a flicker of happiness in the midst of our ongoing grief. We knew the road ahead would be fraught with emotional challenges, but we also knew that we had to take it one day at a time, just as Danielle's father, Robert, had always advised us.

The following months were a whirlwind of travel and family visits, taking us back to the East Coast to see Danielle's father. At 93, Robert was a man of great wisdom and resilience, a proud veteran of the Korean War, and a devoted father to nine children. Our visit to Springfield, Massachusetts, was tinged with the bittersweet recognition that Robert's time was nearing its end. We were grateful that he could meet his grandchild, even if it was only through the presence of the life growing within Danielle. We knew when we returned home that day, that it was likley the last time we would see him on Earth.

Unfortunately, we were correct. Robert would pass just weeks after our visit, marking another significant loss in our lives. He had lived a long, full life, but that didn't make saying goodbye any easier. As we attended his celebration of life, we carried the weight of our grief, not only for Violet and the miscarriage, but now for the loss of a beloved father and grandfather. His words, "Take each day as it comes and make the best of it," echoed in our hearts as we faced the difficult reality of moving forward without him.

ROBERT PANDOLI
03/11/30 – 11/5/23
KOREAN WAR VETERAN – AIR FORCE

During this sorrow, the new life growing inside Danielle was a beacon of hope. It reminded us that even in the darkest of seasons, there is the potential for renewal, for life to spring forth from the depths of despair. As we navigated this pregnancy, we did so with the knowledge of how fragile life can be. We sought out the best care possible, consulting with top specialists in Beverly Hills and taking every precaution to ensure that this time, we would bring our baby home. The trips back and forth through Los Angeles were exhausting, yet they were a pilgrimage of hope, a journey that symbolized our unwavering commitment to this new life. Each visit to the doctor, each ultrasound, was filled with both relief and trepidation. When we heard the reassuring words that there were no signs of vasa previa, we felt a weight lift off our shoulders. This pregnancy, this new beginning, was free from the shadow of the past.

I was beyond eager to learn the gender of our baby, but Danielle had other plans. She reminded me of how we had found out the gender with Violet and expressed her desire for a surprise this time. Though I may have been slightly disappointed, I knew that this was a moment where I had to step back and let her decide. After all we had been through, the least I could do was concede this win to my queen.

As we prepared for the arrival of our baby, we couldn't help but reflect on the journey that had brought us to this point. From the deep sorrow of loss to the cautious hope of a new beginning, we had been through so much. Yet, in all of it, we found that love, in its many forms, was the constant thread that wove our lives together. This chapter is a testament to that love, to the resilience of the human spirit, and to the belief that even in the darkest of times, there is always the possibility of light. We all carry with us the memory of those we have lost and the hope for those we have yet to meet. This book is not just a story of our grief; it is a story for all of us, a story of life in all its seasons. It is a life that continues to unfold, bringing with it both sorrow and joy, loss and renewal, and above all, an enduring love that transcends time and space.

Coping Tools – The Magic of Nostalgia

As I sit here reflecting on the past two years, one of the most surprising yet impactful coping tools I've leaned on has been rekindling an old love affair, my lifelong passion for the Orlando Magic. If you are not into sports, you may want to scroll through this section. For some folks, sports might seem like a trivial escape, a distraction from the real work of healing. For me, this is about much more than just basketball. It's about reconnecting with a piece of my childhood, a time when the world seemed more straightforward, and joy was as easy to find as a game on the local court. Part of the journey of becoming a parent is reflecting on our own parents and childhood.

Growing up in central Florida, football and baseball were the dominant sports, but my heart belonged to basketball. Despite Tampa having professional teams in the three other major sports, the nearest NBA team was 90 minutes away in Orlando. The Orlando Magic began their journey in 1989, and I was there for every moment, captivated by the energy and potential of a new franchise in a league that was exploding in popularity. I was just a kid when the Magic drafted Shaquille O'Neal and Penny Hardaway, transforming a fledgling team into instant contenders. It was a thrilling time to be a young fan, and my dedication to the Magic was absolute.

Danielle likely feels that my heart will never fully belong to her because it's been tethered to the Magic since I was a boy. She's not entirely wrong. I've never missed a game, thanks to the miracle of VCRs in the early days and now the convenience of digital streaming. There's something almost sacred about the ritual of following a team through its ups and downs. For me, the Magic represents not just a team but the best parts of my childhood, the excitement, the hope, and the endless possibilities that came with every tip-off.

I'll never forget the first and only time I saw them play live as a teen. It was January 10, 1994, and my father had saved up to take me to the Orlando Arena. It was my first time attending a professional sporting event of any kind and I was pumped. Shaq and the Magic were facing off against the Houston Rockets, and it felt like a dream come true. The Magic won that day, and for a young boy who had grown up idolizing these players, it was the best day of my life. The irony, of course, is that later that year, these same two teams met in the NBA Finals, and let's just say, the results weren't as kind to my beloved Magic. They lost the series in epic fashion, getting swept by Houston, 4 games to none. Shaq would end up on the Lakers shortly after and the Los Angeles would win a few rings, while Orlando is one of 10 teams to not win a championship yet.

Fast forward a few decades, and here I am, still cheering for a team that has had more than its fair share of rebuilding seasons. But something magical is happening again. The Magic are once again led by young, talented stars, and watching them compete has been a welcome distraction during these tough times. With a game almost every other night from October to May, it's been something to look forward to, a way to lose myself in the familiar rhythms of the sport I love.

There's a certain poetry in sports that I've come to appreciate even more as I've gotten older. It's not just about the scores or the stats; it's about the memories and the emotions that these games evoke. Watching the Magic play takes me back to those simpler times, to the excitement of my youth, and it provides a comforting escape from the complexities of adult life. It's a reminder that some passions never fade, no matter how much time passes.

As we navigate through the grief and challenges of the past few years, this resurgence of the Magic has coincided with some of the most significant moments in my life. Their growth and potential seem to mirror our journey of hope and healing. Even though Danielle might not be as thrilled with my attempts to name our child "O'Neal" or "Orlando" if it is a boy. She understands the joy and the distraction that this team brings me, especially during those moments when we're faced with solitude and reflection.

The Magic's journey has paralleled my own in unexpected ways. Both have experienced their share of rebuilding seasons, periods of struggle and uncertainty, yet both continue to press forward, driven by hope and the promise of what could be. In many ways, this connection to the team has been a grounding force, reminding me that life, like sports, is full of ups and downs, victories, and defeats. It's a constant reminder that even when the odds seem stacked against you, there is always a new season, a new chance to rebuild and grow.

I highly recommend revisiting an old hobby or passion, whether it's watching your favorite sports team, picking up an instrument, collecting sports cards, or diving into a beloved book series. It's not about escaping reality but reconnecting with a part of yourself that brings happiness and comfort. For me, the Orlando Magic has been a source of nostalgia, a reminder of the continuity of life and the enduring power of loyalty and passion. As I look forward to the next chapter, both for the team and in our lives, I'm reminded that even in the midst of grief and loss, there is always room for joy, hope, and the simple pleasures that make life worth living.

Reconnecting with the Magic has also been a way to honor the past while embracing the present. It's a way to acknowledge where I've been, where I am, and where I'm going. The games, the memories, and the community of fellow fans have provided a sense of belonging, a reminder that I'm part of something larger than myself. This connection to the past, to the things that brought me joy as a child, has been a powerful tool in my healing process. It's a reminder that even in the face of profound loss, there is still joy to be found, still memories to be made, and still hope for the future.

Journal Journey – Thanksgiving 2023

We're still hurting, but I can sense a shift, something small but significant, like a tiny crack of light in a very dark room. I'm trying harder to be patient, to keep things light, and to bring back the smiles and laughter that have been so rare these past months. Danielle's well-being, both physically and mentally, is pretty much my main focus right now. Everything I do seems to revolve around her, around us, and around figuring out how to find some solid ground to stand on again.

This time of year, which used to be all about joy and celebration, is now overshadowed by the gaping absence of Violet and Danielle's dad, Robert. Their loss hangs over everything, but it also brings a weird kind of perspective. Thanksgiving has become this complicated mix of pain and gratitude. We're trying to find the right balance between honoring the grief that's still so heavy and making room for whatever healing might be starting to happen. It's not easy. It's like walking a tightrope where you're constantly on edge, trying not to fall into despair while also trying to see if there's any light at the end of this.

Giving thanks this year felt different, like a necessity more than a tradition. It's one way I've found to focus on the little things, the tiny victories that show we're inching forward, even if it doesn't always feel like it. This whole period has been about more than just getting by; it's about trying to nurture these fragile bits of recovery that are starting to poke through the cracks. Healing isn't some big, dramatic event. It's slow, frustratingly slow, and it's in the smallest things, a laugh that actually feels good, a hug that lasts a little longer, or just sitting in silence and not feeling completely broken for a minute.

Thanksgiving 2023 has shown me that we're tougher than I sometimes think, even if the progress feels like it's crawling. It's a reminder that healing is a process, not something you suddenly arrive at. As I write this, it hits me that I'm not just jotting down what's happened, I'm trying to make sense of it, to find some hope in all of this. For anyone going through something similar, healing has these little turning points, some that you notice, some that just sneak up on you. Every step is hard, but they all add up.

The support we've gotten from friends, family, and everyone who's stood by us, it's meant everything. Each text, each small gesture, has reminded us that we're not in this alone. You've helped us find some relief from this crushing grief, and you've shown us just how powerful a simple act of kindness can be. Your support has been the anchor that's kept us from drifting too far into the dark, and for that, we're beyond grateful. As we move forward, I'll remember Thanksgiving 2023 as a marker on this crazy, winding road we're on, a road filled with pain but also with little bits of healing and love. We're still in it, still figuring it out, but I think we're going to make it. We are more grateful every day.

Good Advice – Go For It

It's has been 18 months since Violet passed, and her loss has left a profound mark on every part of my life. Through the heartache and the anger, I've found something unexpected, a newfound fearlessness. I've always been ambitious, driven by a desire to achieve and make an impact. But this was different. This wasn't just ambition; it was a sense of urgency, a realization that I'd already faced some of the worst life could throw at me. I had nothing left to lose by trying, and that realization was liberating. I stopped worrying about what critics might say, about the possibility of failure. I just went for it.

This shift in mindset drove me to seize every opportunity that came my way. Whether it was applying for board positions, recording podcast episodes, volunteering for numerous community roles, or chasing after prestigious scholarships, I didn't hold back. I didn't say no to a single trip or weekend getaway. I simply refused to let life pass me by. I embraced every chance to do something new, to push myself, to make the most of the time I have.

Writing this book is another example of that relentless pursuit. I know that all 50 of my book sales will likely be to supportive friends and family, but if even five people who are struggling, especially those who have known the profound pain of losing a child, find comfort or strength within these pages, that's a victory beyond measure. My new mindset, this "go for it" attitude, has become a cornerstone of how I approach life now. It's about taking the leap, putting myself out there, and embracing the possibilities, no matter how uncertain they might be.

Violet's passing stripped away the illusions of safety and certainty. It taught me that life is fragile, unpredictable, and fleeting. So why not go for it? Why not chase after those dreams, those ideas that seem just out of reach? Why not volunteer, apply, submit, speak, travel, create? The worst that can happen is failure, but even failure becomes a lesson, a steppingstone to something greater. The pain of regret is far worse than the sting of failure.

Following my own advice to "go for it" led me to some incredible opportunities. I was fortunate enough to win scholarships to Stanford's

Local Government Summer Institute in 2023 and the Harvard Kennedy School's State and Local Government Executives program in the summer of 2024. These experiences were life-changing, especially for someone like me, who was kicked out of several colleges in my early 20s. Being on those prestigious campuses, learning from world-class professors, and engaging in cutting-edge conversations was nothing short of surreal. The connections I made in these programs were invaluable and proved incredibly useful as I begun interviewing for me next big role.

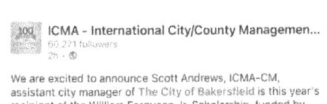

When you "go for it," when you push past your fears and doubts, incredible things can happen. The key is to take that leap, to apply, to put yourself out there because the rewards can be life changing. 'Going for it" is about more than just ambition. It's about living with intention, with the understanding that life is too short to hold back.

It's about embracing the opportunities that come your way, even when they seem daunting. It's about recognizing that every step you take, every risk you embrace, brings you closer to the person you're meant to be. So, go for it! The world is full of possibilities waiting to be explored.

Lessons Learned – Balancing Act

Here's the flip side, the cautionary tale that I learned the hard way: Overcommitting can be just as dangerous as under-committing. In my eagerness to occupy my mind, stay busy, and make every moment count, I bit off more than I could chew. I threw myself into every board, every project, every opportunity that came my way, thinking that staying busy would be the best way to cope with my grief and depression. It turns out that wasn't the case.

Depression has a way of creeping up on you, hitting in strong waves when you least expect it. When my plate was too full, I found myself overwhelmed, stretched too thin, and unable to keep up with the commitments I'd made. I was trying to do it all, but instead of thriving, I was barely surviving. It's not a good look to come off as the hot mess express, especially when people know you're grieving. It was a tough lesson to learn, but an important one. I realized that prioritizing my family and mental well-being had to come first.

I wasn't at 100% in 2023, and I absolutely own that. As we navigated our subsequent pregnancies and the challenges that came with them, it became clear that I couldn't maintain the pace I'd set for myself. We were sleeping maybe two hours a night before our son came home from the hospital, and that exhaustion only made everything harder. It wasn't sustainable. Something had to give.

I made a change. I stepped away from most of my commitments, learning to say "no" to new board opportunities and projects that didn't align with my priorities. Instead, I chose to focus on my professional development, something that was giving me new life and helping me feel like myself again. Each time I completed a leadership program, I felt a renewed sense of purpose, a reminder that I was still growing, still capable of achieving great things, despite the heartache.

This balancing act, learning when to go for it and when to step back, became even more critical when I wasn't 100%. It taught me that while it's important to seize opportunities, it's equally important to know your limits. Prioritizing what truly matters, whether it's your family, your mental health, or your professional growth, is essential for long-term success and well-being. It's about finding that equilibrium, that sweet spot where you're pushing yourself just enough to grow, but not so much that you're risking burnout.

So, here's the lesson learned: Go for it, but don't overextend yourself. Know when to say yes and when to say no. It's a delicate balance, but one that's necessary if you want to thrive rather than just survive. Life is short, and it's up to us to make the most of it. That doesn't mean we have to burn ourselves out in the process. Find your balance, pursue your passions, and remember that it's okay to step back, to rest, and to focus on what truly matters. In doing so, you'll find the strength and resilience to keep moving forward, even in the face of life's greatest challenges.

CHAPTER 9

Fuzzy

The first few chapters of this book reflect our shared journey, but they unmistakably resonate more with my voice, my perspective. This chapter is focused more on Fuzzy. The nickname that came about because her demeanor is always so warm and fuzzy. Danielle, my better half, is much more private than I am, and in many ways, my healing process, marked by journaling and now, by this book, stands in stark contrast to hers. As a multi-time nominee for "Husband of the Year," I've yet to bring home the top prize, probably because I share more than Danielle is comfortable with. It's just one of my many less-than-lovely traits that keeps me from that coveted award. And yes, there's some sarcasm in that, but it's also very true.

Let me tell you about my favorite person in the world and her healing journey. Danielle is a kind soul who gives everyone the benefit of the doubt. She not only feeds off other people's energy but also serves as a sounding board, absorbing all that they're experiencing. She is the CEO (Chief Empathetic Officer) of my world. If you don't believe that people can be true empaths, I'd like to introduce Exhibit A: my beautiful wife, Danielle. The challenge for her, as an empath, is that she carries all the grief and depression that I've endured, plus her own. Let's not forget the hormones and powerful emotions that only mothers can truly understand, emotions amplified tenfold by the loss of our little girl, the miscarriage that followed, and her role as the emotional anchor of our family. I'm telling you, this woman is a saint.

Danielle rarely complains, but when things get really tough, she internalizes her pain, sharing it only with a select few. It was incredibly difficult for me to return to work just two weeks after Violet passed, but I can't even begin to fathom what it was like for Danielle to stay home all day, in a place we had only lived for six months. For a loving, pediatric critical care nurse like her, I imagine it was torturous. While I may not have felt like socializing at work, at least I had the option. This is a far cry from me, the outwardly strong but vulnerable megaphone. My approach has always been to share, in the hope that it might help someone in need. This method has come with some very hard lessons for me over the last two years.

As I reflect on our journey, I am reminded daily of Danielle's incredible strength. Her quiet resilience has been the foundation of our family's healing. While I poured my emotions onto these pages, she held space for us all, absorbing our pain and turning it into love and support. Danielle, with her boundless empathy, navigated through the darkest days with a grace that can only be described as saintly. She embodied the very essence of unconditional love and showed me that healing is not just about sharing our grief but also about finding comfort in each other's presence. Her role as the Chief Empathetic Officer of our family is not just a title, but a testament to her unwavering dedication and love.

Our home, filled with memories of Violet, became a sanctuary of healing because of Danielle. She transformed a place of sorrow into a haven of hope, not just for herself but for all of us. Her ability to listen, to empathize, and to support without asking for anything in return has been nothing short of miraculous. In those moments when I struggled to find my way, Danielle was there, a beacon of light guiding me back. She never wavered, even when her own heart was breaking. Her strength gave me the courage to continue sharing our story, to turn our pain into a message of hope and resilience.

I have been blown away by how Danielle managed to juggle her emotions through a nearly perfect pregnancy with Violet. Then, we had the tragedy of losing Violet, almost dying herself, and then coming back to be pregnant again. The miscarriage after loss shattered her hope for a while, which is saying a lot. Then, we were on eggshells, and she was sleeping even less than we do now, while we were pregnant for the third time. She had to say goodbye to her father while pregnant. I cant imagine how hard that was for her while her internal chemistry was already in shock. The mental fortitude she has displayed is incredible. I am in awe of how she accomplishes all of this while being a supportive wife, being there for me during my own struggles, and choosing to trust in God again.

Through all of her tears and heartache, we shared so many laughs. We traveled to countless places together, discovering new countries and embarking on new adventures. These experiences were not just escapes but testaments to our resilience and our commitment to living fully despite our losses. Each journey was a new chapter in our shared life, a testament to our love for each other and our determination to move forward despite the pain.

Danielle's resilience isn't just about surviving; it's about thriving in the face of adversity. After the loss of Violet, Danielle found the strength to support me, even when she was dealing with her own grief. She never let her pain overshadow her love for our family. She chose to see the beauty in life, even when it was hard to find. Her faith in God and her belief in the goodness of people helped her navigate the darkest days.

Our shared experiences, from the highs of travel and discovery to the lows of loss, grief, and depression, have only strengthened our bond. Danielle's unwavering support and love have been my anchor. Her ability to find joy and strength in the face of adversity is a testament to her incredible character. She is not just my wife; she is my partner in crime, my shipmate, my soulmate, my everything. Through all the highs and lows, we've had the privilege of laughing together, crying together, and growing together. These experiences have enriched our lives and provided us with beautiful memories to cherish forever. She found a way to rise above it, to find hope and joy again.

I am filled with gratitude for the journey we have walked together. Danielle, my rock and my inspiration, has shown me that true healing is found in love, in the quiet moments of understanding, in the shared tears, and in the strength, we find in each other. Together, we honor Violet's memory by living fully, loving deeply, and finding gratitude and joy in the little moments. It turns out the little moments are the big moments. Thank you, Danielle, for being the heart and soul of our family. Thank you for showing me what true strength looks like.

Coping Tool: Writing and Journaling

In the quiet spaces of my life, amidst the chaos of grief and the relentless demands of my career, I found an unexpected sanctuary in writing. Journaling became more than just a coping tool; it became a lifeline, a way to navigate the turbulent seas of loss and depression. This practice wasn't new to me, I'd been journaling on and off since my early twenties, following the advice of a mentor who recognized that my mind was always brimming with ideas, emotions, and the occasional wacky thought. But it wasn't until the last few years, as Danielle and I built our life together and as my career climbed new heights, that I truly realized the power of putting pen to paper.

I've always embraced my creative side, and with that comes a flood of ideas, some brilliant, some...not so much. The challenge, I discovered, was capturing those ideas before they slipped away. Not every idea is a winner, much like in baseball, where a .300 batting average makes you a Hall-of-Famer, not every thought needs to be a home run. Journaling allowed me to capture those ideas, to sift through them, and occasionally, to hit one out of the park. This process has been incredibly cathartic, helping me to manage the balancing act between my personal life and a demanding career.

Writing became my way of processing the highs and lows, of reflecting on the moments that mattered. It was in these moments of reflection that I began to see the real value of journaling, not just as a tool for creativity, but as a means of tracking my growth over time. Looking back on entries from months or even years ago, I could see the progress I'd made, the challenges I'd overcome, and the person I was becoming. It was a way to measure growth that often goes unnoticed in the day-to-day grind of life.

But journaling wasn't just about looking back; it was also about finding a way forward. When the weight of grief became too heavy to bear, writing provided a release. It gave me a space to express the deepest fears and longings of my heart, thoughts that I couldn't, or wouldn't, speak aloud. It became a bridge to my inner self, a way to articulate the inarticulable. Through writing, I found clarity in the chaos, peace in the storm.

And something remarkable happened when I began to share my reflections. Writing became not just a personal practice, but a way to connect with others. By sharing my thoughts, I demystified my experiences, granting friends, family, and colleagues a window into my world. It allowed them to walk beside me on this journey in a way that spoken words couldn't. Writing brought people closer to me, fostering understanding and empathy, and creating a sense of community around the struggles I was facing.

In encouraging others to try journaling, I'd say this: You don't have to be a poet or a novelist to find value in writing. Sometimes, my entries are as simple as to-do lists, brainstorms, or random ideas. It's not about perfection; it's about expression. It's about giving yourself permission to feel, to think, and to grow. Writing is a powerful tool for anyone navigating the complexities of life. It's a way to honor your thoughts, to capture the fleeting moments, and to build a bridge between your inner world and the world around you.

So, grab a pen, open a journal, and start writing. Let it be messy, let it be raw, let it be real. Whether you're chronicling your day, processing your emotions, or dreaming up your next big idea, the act of writing can be a transformative experience. It's a practice that has not only helped me to heal but has also reminded me of the power of my own voice. In a world that often feels overwhelming, that's a gift worth embracing.

Writing has become more than just a coping mechanism; it's become an integral part of how I navigate the world. When life feels like it's spinning out of control, writing provides a sense of order, a way to make sense of the chaos. It's a space where I can be completely honest, where there are no expectations, and where I can explore the depths of my thoughts and emotions without fear of judgment. Journaling has been a tool for self-discovery, a way to uncover parts of myself that I didn't even know existed.

In these pages, I've found a mirror reflecting not just my struggles, but also my strengths. It's where I've been able to confront my fears, celebrate my victories, and find peace in the midst of turmoil. Through writing, I've learned to appreciate the small moments, to find beauty in the ordinary, and to stay connected to what truly matters. It's taught me to be patient with myself, to understand that healing is not a linear process, and to embrace the journey, no matter how difficult it may be.

If you've ever felt lost, overwhelmed, or disconnected, I encourage you to try journaling. It doesn't matter if your words are messy or if your thoughts are scattered. What matters is that you give yourself the space to express whatever is in your heart. Let writing be your sanctuary, a place where you can find solace, strength, and the courage to keep moving forward. Because sometimes, the simple act of putting pen to paper can be the most powerful tool for healing.

Journal Journey – Meeting Jada

In the shimmering heat of Phoenix, under a sky that seemed to stretch endlessly, we stood on the threshold of a moment that had loomed large in our hearts and minds, both anticipated and quietly feared. Our hearts felt the weight of what was and the tender hopes of what might be, as we prepared to meet "Jada," the beautiful daughter of our close friends, born on the same day as Violet. The symmetry of these events, their daughter's birth alongside our agonizing loss, had etched itself into our consciousness, a constant reminder of life's fragility. The thought of meeting Jada had become a mixture of trepidation and longing, a mental and emotional storm we knew we needed to face.

As we approached their home, I felt the pressure of the moment tightening around me, a knot of fear and anticipation that swirled in my chest. How would we react? How could we hold this precious child, a living reminder of the daughter we lost, without breaking down? These questions circled endlessly, but there was a resolve between us: this was an essential step in our healing journey, one we had to take, no matter how difficult.

When we arrived, something extraordinary happened. Jada's innocent joy cut through the tension like a warm ray of sunlight. With a child's unfiltered enthusiasm, she ran toward us, her arms outstretched in a welcoming embrace that took us by surprise. In that moment, it was as if the universe itself was speaking to us, reminding us that love, in its purest form, transcends the boundaries of loss and sorrow. Her small arms seemed to carry a touch of the divine, a gentle reminder that even in our deepest grief, there is room for connection and hope.

As I held Jada close, tears welled up, tears not of sadness, but of profound gratitude. Her guileless joy was like a balm to our wounded hearts, a living symbol of hope and connection. In that tender embrace, I felt something beyond the physical, a whisper from Violet herself, as though she was reaching out to us through Jada. It was a gentle affirmation from the daughter we still long to hold, reminding us that she is never truly gone, that her spirit lives on in the love we share and the lives we touch.

The moment that had loomed so large in our minds, the moment we had both dreaded and longed for, arrived and unfolded differently than we had imagined. Instead of the heartache we feared, we found something entirely unexpected: peace. Jada wasn't a painful reminder of what we had lost; she was a beacon of what lies ahead. Holding her in our arms, we didn't feel the sharp sting of grief but rather the warmth of possibility, the comfort of knowing that life continues, that love persists, even in the face of loss.

This encounter, which had built up so much emotional weight in our minds, became a milestone in our journey, a step closer to the future we were cautiously hopeful for. Jada, with her bright eyes and innocent laughter, wasn't a mirror reflecting our loss; she was a light guiding us forward, a reminder that the world still holds beauty and promise. In that moment, our hearts were fortified by an unexpected grace, a sense of peace that had eluded us for so long.

As we left Phoenix, we carried with us not just the memory of meeting Jada, but a renewed sense of purpose and hope. What we had once feared became a turning point, a testament to the power of connection, to the healing that can come from the most unexpected places, and to the enduring presence of love in every form it chooses to reveal itself. With this encounter, we felt more ready than ever to welcome a new life into our arms, less than three weeks away from holding our third child.

Thus, this experience finds its place within the pages of *Violet's Are Blue*, a chapter that speaks to the resilience of the human spirit, the beauty of unexpected connections. In meeting Jada, we didn't just confront the child we had lost; we embraced the future we were beginning to envision, a future filled with hope, love, and the promise of new beginnings. This moment reminded us that even in the shadow of loss, there is light, there is life, and there is always, always love.

Lessons Learned - A Piercing Lesson

Starting with her funeral service on January 28, 2023, when we asked everyone to wear violet or purple in lieu of the usual black, Danielle and I have found countless ways to honor Violet in the months since we said goodbye. These gestures, big and small, have brought us moments of peace, comfort, and connection to our daughter. Some, however, have been a stretch of well-intentioned but misguided attempts that, in hindsight, may have caused more heartache than healing.

Let me start by saying I now own more purple items than Willy Wonka. I've always been confident, bordering on splashy, with my style choices, but my wardrobe has taken on a whole new hue. Two shades of purple blazers, multiple pairs of violet sneakers, dress shirts, casual shirts, gym clothes, the list goes on. I'm serious when I say Barney and Grimace have nothing on my collection. In all honesty, wearing purple has been incredibly therapeutic for me. As silly as it may sound to others, I feel a sense of closeness to Violet when I'm wrapped in her color. It's like a comforting embrace, a subtle reminder that she's always with me, woven into the fabric of my daily life.

Over the past year, we've received more potted violets than we can count, at least six of them. Unfortunately, five of those met an untimely end thanks to our feisty felines. Beyond the tangible tributes, we've explored other, less conventional means of connecting with Violet. In our desperation to feel close to her, we even consulted a psychic medium. I know some might frown upon this, but in the weeks following our loss, we were grasping at anything that might bring us closer to her. The sessions were a mix of fantastic, freaky, and frightening, and while they weren't for us long-term, they did offer a brief sense of comfort. I carried a purple gem stone from the medium in my pocket for months until I had my dedication tattoo for Violet completed in June of '23.

Speaking of the enormous tattoo, covering the majority of my leg. It's more than just ink on skin. It is a testament to the unbreakable bond between a father, a mother, and their angel child. Etched upon my leg are Violet's hand and footprints, captured in life-sized detail, along with an image of Danielle holding her. Above this, Violet is imagined with wings, a symbol of her purity and peace. Her name, Violet Françoise, flows in elegant script, a whisper of beauty and grief intertwined. This tattoo is not merely a marking; it's a canvas of the soul, an emblem of the promises whispered, the dreams held, and the moments too brief. It's a permanent reminder of the love we will always carry for our daughter.

As meaningful as these gestures have been, not all of our attempts to honor Violet have gone as smoothly. Case in point: the ill-advised decision to re-pierce my ears during what would have been Violet's first birthday week. Let me take you back to the mid-90s when I sported earrings everywhere until the age of 26. As I stepped up my professionalism, I started wearing them only "off the clock," and eventually, I stopped altogether when I earned my first assignment in city management. At the one-year mark of her death, in a moment of grief-fueled sadness, I thought it would be symbolic, even cool, to re-pierce my ears as a way to honor Violet, something I had hoped to do with her one day.

Well, let me tell you, this was a terrible idea. I rushed out the door, had my ears pierced, and had forgotten that you're supposed to leave the earrings in for six to eight weeks. I tried to hide them at work with clear plastic studs, but I started pulling them in and out based on my meetings, which led to infection and swollen earlobes. Super sexy, right? Needless to say, everyone noticed, including my most outspoken councilmember, who commented on my new look. I looked like a cross between a grieving father and someone who's a red, convertible Corvette away from a full-fledged mid-life crisis. It was not a good look.

So, if you're reading this and considering a symbolic gesture to honor a loved one, especially if you're over 40, take it from me: steer clear of the piercing route. There's definitely a duality in grief, the private mourning that seeks solace in solitude, and the outward expressions that yearn for understanding. While the tattoo and the purple attire have been comforting, the earrings? Not so much. It turns out that wearing your heart on your sleeve, or in this case, your ear—doesn't always go as planned.

In the end, grief is a journey marked by moments of deep introspection and some less-than-stellar decisions. But through it all, we find ways to honor our loved ones, to keep their memory alive, and to navigate the pain with grace, or at least with a sense of humor. So, I choose to continue sharing our story of love, loss, and the enduring bond we share with Violet. But I'll leave the mid-life crisis earring lesson as a cautionary tale for others.

Through these experiences, I've learned that it's okay to try and find comfort in unconventional ways, even if they don't always work out as planned. The important thing is that we continue to seek connection with those we've lost, even if it means making a few mistakes along the way. Every gesture, whether it brings comfort or just a chuckle, is a part of the healing process, and it's all part of the journey of keeping our loved ones close, in whatever way we can.

Good Advice – Date Nights

In the days following Violet's passing, our world shrank to the size of our living room. The thought of socializing felt overwhelming, and some days, even the effort of getting dressed seemed too much to bear. We cocooned ourselves in our grief, allowing the silence and sorrow to wash over us. The walls of our home became both a refuge and a reminder of the life we had lost. Yet, as the weeks turned into months, a quiet need began to stir, a need to reconnect with life, with each other, and with the world beyond our front door.

This led us back to one of the simplest yet most profound rituals of any relationship: date nights. These evenings became our lifeline, a bridge between the life we had known and the life we were trying to rebuild. They weren't just about getting out of the house or filling our time; they were intentional acts of love, spaces where we could breathe, talk, laugh, and just be together. In a world that suddenly felt foreign, date nights were a way to reclaim some semblance of normalcy.

In the quiet corners of restaurants, over shared plates and stolen glances, we found pieces of ourselves that had been buried under the weight of grief. The act of dressing up, of choosing a place to go, of anticipating a meal we didn't have to cook, these small acts became significant. They were declarations that life, though altered, was still worth living, that joy could still be found even in the midst of sorrow. It wasn't just about the food or the ambiance; it was about the connection that had been dulled by the haze of loss.

For us, these date nights weren't just about the food, though as self-proclaimed foodies, that was certainly a highlight. It was about the connection. It was about leaning into each other when everything else felt uncertain. We realized that with a new baby on the way, our opportunities for quiet, uninterrupted moments together would soon become even rarer. So, we seized these nights with a renewed appreciation, knowing they were moments to be savored. Each date night became a small victory, a reminder that we were still standing, still fighting for our love and our future.

There's a certain magic in rediscovering your partner through shared experiences, in remembering why you fell in love in the first place. The candlelight, the clinking of glasses, the hushed conversations, they all created a space where we could momentarily set aside our worries and simply enjoy each other's company. In those moments, the world outside ceased to exist. It was just us, a team, navigating the waves of grief and preparing for the unknowns that lay ahead. These evenings served as a reminder that, even in the darkest of times, there is light to be found in each other's presence.

As we edge closer to the arrival of our son/daughter in March, the anxiety is mounting. These date nights have provided a counterbalance, a way to ground ourselves in the present and remind us of the strength we draw from each other. They've been a reminder that, no matter what happens, we have each other to lean on. In a time when it felt like the ground could shift beneath us at any moment, these nights out together became the anchors that kept us steady.

For anyone walking through a season of struggle, I cannot emphasize enough the importance of prioritizing time with your partner. It's easy to let the weight of the world keep you home, to convince yourself that it's easier not to go out, not to make the effort. But in truth, these moments of intentional connection can be a lifeline. They allow you to step away from the heaviness of your circumstances and to remember the love that brought you together in the first place. It's in these shared moments that you can rediscover the joy that might feel so distant.

In these pages, as we share our journey of loss, love, and healing, I hope you find inspiration to create your own moments of reprieve. Whether it's a night out on the town or a quiet dinner at home, make time for each other. Lean into the love you share and allow it to be the balm that soothes your soul. My advice: it's these simple, intentional moments that remind us of the enduring strength found within the bonds of love. It's in these moments that we find not only the courage to face another day but also the hope that brighter days are still ahead.

CHAPTER 10

Our Fairy a Miles of Joy Tale

We were nearing the finish line. Our scheduled C-section was set for March 19, 2024, and we couldn't wait to meet our baby. The last ten weeks of the pregnancy were heavy, both emotionally and physically. Stress eating became a reality, and the anticipation of the big day had us on edge. The final three weeks crept along at a snail's pace, raising anxiety with each passing day. We were tense, sometimes even with each other, but we knew we were in this together. Danielle had a fantastic support system with her grief groups, mom's groups, book clubs, and amazing neighbors who have become lifelong friends. Despite the absence of Violet, our lives were still filled with abundance.

I found my own ways to stay busy, diving into projects, professional development, and books. Yet, I have to admit, irritability stew was a regular dish served in our home. The recipe wasn't complex; just three hours of sleep, a scoop of depression, a cup of anxiety, and stir on high heat. Ready or not, it was served. Even through the challenges, we got through it, just as we always do. Finally, the big day arrived. After seeking multiple opinions on our baby's health, we opted to deliver locally, despite the emotional weight of returning to the same hospital where we said goodbye to Violet just 14 months earlier. It was tormenting to be there, but it made the most sense for our family. We had built a strong rapport with our doctor and medical team, and our close friends were even in the waiting room, just like in the movies.

We learned that the child following the loss of a baby is often called a "rainbow baby." As we prepared to meet ours, we played the beautiful, powerful lyrics of popstar, Casey Musgraves' "Rainbow" in the hospital during the C-section. The medical team had already started the procedure before Danielle even realized. She was physically numb even as her emotions runneth over. I watched as our 8-pound baby was handed to me, and with shock and elation, I announced, "I want you to meet Miles." Danielle had been convinced we were having a girl, so she thought I was teasing until she saw our beautiful baby boy for herself.

Our 8 lb Miles provided us a scare when he entered the world as well. He swallowed a lot of fluid during birth and would be admitted for two very long days. We were in pure agony as his ICU bed was only about 20 feet away from where we said goodbye to Violet the year before. Vio was watching over us though and Miles would bounce back fast. We would load him up in the car seat, where I proceeded to drive 20 mph the whole way home.

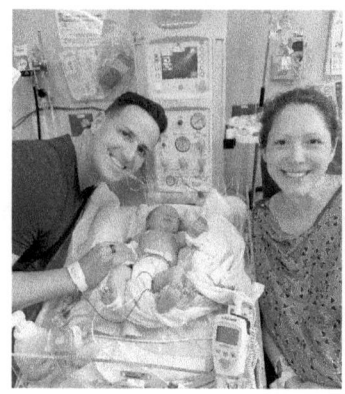

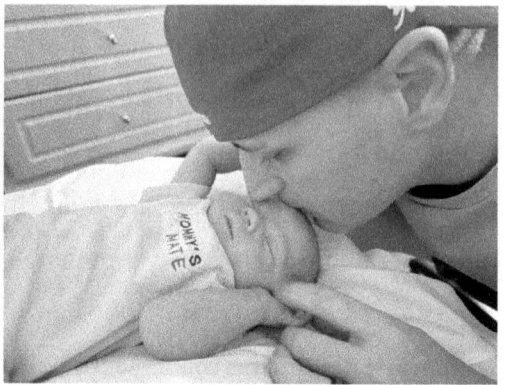

Miles Robert Andrews, or as I like to call him, "my main man Miles." We had a few disagreements over names, but Miles felt right. It was cool, cultured, and has a touch of sophistication. It also reflected our love for travel, a nod to the many miles we would journey together as a family. Choosing the middle name took a bit longer, but with the decline and eventual passing of Danielle's father, Robert Pandoli, the decision became clear. Robert is also the name of a beloved family member on my side. Robert Scott is my great uncle and sister to my beloved grandmother Violet. It is surreal to think that two generations later, another Violet and Robert are part of our family. It's as if life has come full circle.

Violet will always be the angel watching over Miles, sheltering us with her love. We believe she brought him to us. We lovingly call him our lucky charm, born the week of St. Patrick's Day with his Irish heritage shining through. Miles is our pride and joy. Even at five months old, I can already see some of my traits in him. Genetics are fascinating, and he looked so much like me as a baby, yet he has Danielle's unmistakable dimple, her delightful signature. After losing Violet and experiencing a miscarriage, I was beginning to lose hope of having a healthy child. I always talked to Danielle's belly during both pregnancies, but deep down, I knew we were having a boy this time. The pregnancy was different, more challenging in terms of pain and discomfort. Danielle's demeanor and cravings were also different.

As a sports enthusiast, the idea of watching games with my son is a dream come true. It is special and nostalgic in every way. Miles' presence has brought a renewed sense of purpose and joy to our lives. His laughter, curiosity, and pure joy remind us of the beauty and resilience of life. Each day with him is a gift, a reminder that after the darkest storms, there is always a sunrise.

Watching Danielle nurse and care for Miles fills me with gratitude. She is an incredible mother, nurturing and loving him with all her heart. Her strength, dedication, and resilience continue to inspire me. We often look back at pictures of ourselves from three to five years ago and see an innocence in those "kids" that we no longer possess. The loss of a child marks a moment in time, creating a "before and after" in your life. The journey through grief and the battle against anxiety and depression have given us a superpower of immense perspective. We no longer take anything for granted. Even the smallest gestures of kindness mean the world to us.

Things that used to be an annoyance seem trivial now. I am much more in sync with my intuition. We feel a deep sense of gratitude for everything positive in our lives. Meeting others who have experienced similar losses creates a new circle of trust and support, a new tribe. Those who have lost recognize and appreciate each other in a profound way. I saw firsthand how these havens of hope helped Danielle find her way back to the surface, swimming to shore with their support. I am indebted to these groups that ask for nothing in return but for you to pay it forward. This book, this journal journey, is my attempt at paying it forward. If our story inspires even five people, it will have been worth it.

To anyone in the depths of depression, keep going. You will make it. Look for the beacons of hope and the signs of light. Whether you call it fate or faith, the hardest battle is within yourself. You will make it when you learn to let your guard down, trust others' intentions, and lean into your healing journey. Colleagues, friends of friends, and even strangers will reach out to you in confidence, sharing their own experiences of loss and struggle. We all wear a mask, reflecting the best version of ourselves, but beneath it, we have all faced challenges. When we give grace, we receive it. Kindness finds kindness. Keep going, take each day as it comes, and make the best of it.

Miles
Robert
8 lbs 0 oz
21 inches
March 19, 2024
TheStorkConnection.com
661-322-1610
Big Sister
Violet
Our Angel
in Heaven

FINAL REFLECTIONS

As of September 2024, this book is complete. I have an immense sense of fulfillment as I prepare to send "Violet's Are Blue" off to the publisher. This project has been a labor of love, comfort and commitment. I wrote different portions of this book over the last two years. As you have experienced, some of the chapters have been difficult to read. They were even harder to write and edit as I would have to take a few weeks off in-between at times. We are approaching what our new "normal" looks like. Although we are convinced that there is no such thing as normal.

Miles is now approaching 6 months old. We did not have a baby shower, but this time we had the baby. It is incredible how hard and how much fun the last few months have been. He is amazing and I can see so much of both of us in him already. Danielle has exceeded all expectations, as usual. She has solely breast-fed Miles thus far, which means feeding him every 2-3 hours, 24/7. My little saint Danielle is absolutely a machine. I have so much respect for parents everywhere, especially all the mothers.

As of June 2024, I hit the two-year mark in my role with the City of Bakersfield. The two-year anniversary of my start date serves as a "code of ethics minimum" in my role. Despite all our challenges in the past two years, I wanted to honor this benchmark. I truly did not think I would be able to stay in our house this long, but we powered through. In the last three weeks I have accepted my first County

Manager role. Danielle, Miles and I will be packing up the fur fam and heading to Las Cruces in the next month as I join Doña Ana County, New Mexico as their next CEO/CAO. Miles will get to grow up in a super diverse, college town, with a high quality of life. More than anything, we will get the fresh start that we so badly need. Violet's parents are no longer blue. We are ready for the joy of the Miles ahead on our journey.

To our friends, family, community, and everyone who has supported us, thank you. Your love and encouragement have meant the world to us. You have helped us find joy amid sorrow and hope in the face of despair. Your support has carried us. I am filled with gratitude for the miracle that is Miles. He is our lucky charm, a testament to the enduring power of love, hope, and faith. Together, we honor Violet's memory by leading our lives with love, being grateful for everything, loving deeply, and finding joy in the little moments.

REFERENCES

Brein, M. (2021). *Traveling and mental health: How exploring the world can heal you.* Psychology Today.

Gump, B. B., & Matthews, K. A. (2018). *Stress, vacation, and well-being: Findings from Austrian middle managers.* Journal of Travel Research.

Jones, H., & He, Q. (2023). *The role of travel in social participation and health: Evidence from the Journal of Transport & Health.* Journal of Transport & Health.

Kahlil Gibran, a philosopher and writer known for his book "The Prophet,"

Milman, A. (2021). *Travel, self-esteem, and life satisfaction: Evidence from recent research.* Personality and Individual Differences.

Smith, K. J., Gall, S. L., McNaughton, S. A., Blizzard, L., Dwyer, T., & Venn, A. J. (2019). *The association between vacation frequency and metabolic syndrome: Findings from the Journal of Psychology & Health.* Psychology & Health.

University of East Anglia. (n.d.). *Vacation and depression risk: A study on the mental health benefits of travel.* University of East Anglia.

Witters, Dan (20203). Depression rates reach new highs. Retrieved from https://news.gallup.com/poll/505745/depression-rates-reach-new-highs.aspx#:~:text=In%202023%2C%2029.0%25%20of%20Americans,Health%20and%20Well%2DBeing%20Index.
World Health Organization. (2023). *The health benefits of travel.* World Health Organization.

Milton Keynes UK
Ingram Content Group UK Ltd.
UKHW021421231024
450026UK00012BA/767

9 781637 927724